The author at the ruins of Gran Pajatén. The angular spirals and stepped-Grecque and zigzag designs are characteristic of ancient Andean structures.

Circular building constructed by the Chachapoyas on the slopes of the eastern Andes between A.D. 800 and 1500. Note the medial moldings and ornamental decorations.

(Opposite, above) The caracole or astronomical observatory of Chichén Itzá, a Maya building with similar medial moldings and angular spirals.

(Below) In Peru the author found these aquatic designs among the ruins of a circular structure.

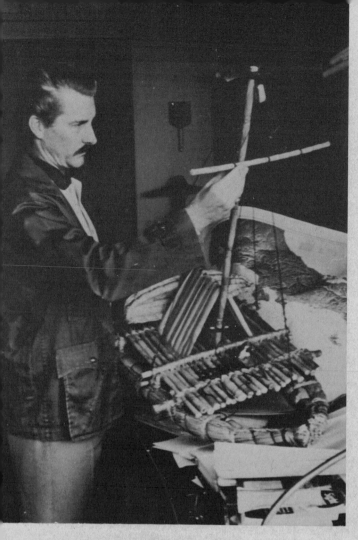

From totora reed and bamboo cane the author builds his first model of the sturdy sailing raft that plied the Peruvian seacoast more than a thousand years ago.

The real raft under construction. The author with José Arzola-Huaman-chumo, Huan-chaquero totora headman.

The bamboo cane deck is lashed into place at Salaverry, Peru.

The first multihulled reed vessel to take to the open sea in many centuries lowers her sweep oar. She is christened the Feathered Serpent.

*Alone on the open
sea off the northern
Peruvian coast.*

Off on the trail of the Feathered Serpent.

ON THE
TRAIL
OF THE
FEATHERED
SERPENT

On the Trail of the Feathered Serpent

Gene Savoy

THE BOBBS-MERRILL COMPANY, INC.
Indianapolis • New York

Illustrations with the exception of those otherwise credited are
by Gene Savoy.

To my good friend and fellow explorer
CARL C. LANDEGGER

ACKNOWLEDGMENTS

The Author wishes to express his gratitude for the generous assistance given by the officers and men of the Naval and Port Authorities of Peru, Ecuador, Panama, and the United States. Special thanks are also hereby extended to the following firms and organizations whose financial and material contributions helped bring about the successful conclusion of the Expedition:

> *El Comercio* Newspaper of Lima, Peru
> The Columbia Broadcasting System
> Faucett Airlines of Peru
> Abercrombie & Fitch of New York
> New York Nautical Instrument Company
> Lafayette Radio Electronics Corporation
> Foto International of Panama
> Kodak of Peru
> LAN-Chile Airlines

Thanks are also extended to the many individuals mentioned below who gave so freely of their time, thereby making a most valuable contribution to the Expedition:

> His Excellency Guillermo Gerberding Melgar, Former Peruvian
>   Ambassador to Panama
> J. W. Higgens, Chamber of Commerce, San Diego
> L. E. Gehres, Master, National Marine Terminal, San Diego
> Alejandro Mendez P., Director, National Monuments, Panama City
> Clinton R. Edwards, Dept. of Geography, University of Wisconsin
> Jaime Casapia, Andean Explorers Club, Lima, Peru
> Anselmo Fukuda, Nikon Representative, Lima, Peru
> Robert L. Bollinger, New Jersey
> Robert E. Harris, Master Sailor, Sydney, Australia
> Captain George Stevens of the SS *Westgate*
> Malcolm Burke, Lima, Peru

I must also give thanks to the Andean Explorers Club, sponsor of the Expedition, and to the many unnamed members and friends whose energies and advice made possible our movements on land and on the sea from Peru to Mexico.

CONTENTS

FOREWORD

The idea of a sea voyage made by aboriginal-type craft first came to me in the jungles of Peru when I noted the similarity between the architectural designs of newly discovered cities and those of Mesoamerica. I was positive there had been contact at one time in history. Though the significance of this contact was of great interest to me, at the time I was more interested in how such a contact had been made. I had uncovered enough jungle roads to know that land routes were a possibility. But maritime contact—that was a fascinating prospect.

Pre-Columbian Americans were coastal seafarers. Their primitive methods of navigation by sun, stars, winds, and currents allowed them to move up and down the shoreline where regular landfalls could be made. This was indicated by Spanish navigators who first sighted rafts and reed floats plying the coasts of Ecuador and Peru. Mayan canoes had been seen sailing along the shoreline of the Caribbean between the Yucatán peninsula, Guatemala, and Honduras, even as far south as Panama. Thus, the evidence indicated that such a trip had been made—and could be made again.

When I approached old sailing masters about my idea of sailing a primitive vessel from Peru to Middle America, they were pessimistic and predicted that any attempt would fail. They suggested that the strong Peruvian or Humboldt current, which flows northward but swings west at Cabo Blanco, would carry the craft to the Galápagos Islands, or more likely to the South Pacific Islands. More probably, it was speculated, the northwest winds that prevail in that area would blow the craft on shore.

Generally speaking, the expedition was made with the intention of supporting my ethnological studies in the eastern forests and demonstrating that ancient peoples of Peru used wind and current to communicate with their neighbors to the north in Ecuador, Colombia, Panama, and Mexico. That sea routes have existed in the past is an idea acceptable to most archaeologists, anthropologists, and cultural geographers. Most scientists with whom I discussed the matter felt that a successful sea expedition would be meaningless; that it would not prove that such trips had been made. Friends felt that my archaeological investigations east of the Andes were making a more valid contribution to our knowledge of pre-Columbian man in South America. While no one actually tried to discourage me from making the trip, most agreed there was no real need to make one.

I did not agree with these opinions. I believed the reconstruction of an aboriginal watercraft from authentic sources, using primitive materials and duplicating all conditions with which ancient mariners had to contend, was a fascinating challenge. I was firmly convinced a coastal route had been used, and with the same determination that had sent me looking for the legendary "lost city of the Incas" a few years before, at a place every archaeologist assured me could not possibly be the site of Vilcabamba, I resolved to find it. As for the logistics, if primitive sailors using crude navigational aids could make a trip like the one I planned, then such a voyage was surely feasible in modern times.

Of course I had other reasons for undertaking the expedition. The upper jungles, the length of Peru east of the Andes, contained evidence of ancient civilizations. Of the more than forty stone temples, ceremonial centers, and cities I had reclaimed from the primordial rain forests, many incorporated into the architecture the concept of a great personage. This historic figure was known to the old Peruvians as Viracocha, among other names. According to legend, he sailed away to the north following a period of persecution. I believed he emerged in Mexico as Quetzalcoatl, the Feathered Serpent.

A successful trip would support my belief that the Peruvian Viracocha and the Mexican Quetzalcoatl were more than likely one and the same person, and that the many other cultural heroes known to us through the folklore of pre-Columbian Americans may be identified with him. That Viracocha sailed north rather than across the Pacific is supported by historical texts centuries old; thus he could not have settled Easter Island.

For years I had trekked along the backbone of the Andes in the footsteps of this mythical hero, down into the steaming jungles and back to the coast again. Now the thought of following his sea travels filled me with enthusiasm. The possibility of bridging the two continents by means of a reconstructed sea voyage, thereby linking up the magnificent monuments of Mesoamerica with those I had discovered in eastern Peru, was a temptation I could not resist.

ON THE
TRAIL
OF THE
FEATHERED
SERPENT

The Challenge

Justifiable Criticism

If I was to get the balsa into the water before April, I would have to hurry. Taking the stairs to the ground floor (in preference to the rickety old elevator), I reached the street, waved down a taxi, and told the driver to take me to the offices of the Andean Explorers Club, where I had stored my gear.

I had approached old sailing masters, those hardy men who sail their diesel-powered tuna clippers up and down the coast from California to Peru, and they were not optimistic about the success of my proposed expedition. They believed that the Humboldt current would carry any cumbersome raft toward the Galápagos if the raft managed to reach as far north as Cabo Blanco. If the prevailing winds from the northwest did not overcome the force of the current, the raft would be driven to the South Pacific Islands. If it sailed closer to shore, the weak southerly counter-current would work against it. The only hope for success was to take advantage of the weak inshore current that traveled into the Bay of Panama. Even then, I was told, in all probability the northwest winds would prevail in the area and blow the craft to shore. I was warned about the winds along the coast, which blow at a steady 50 miles per hour and can very quickly work up a tremendous short sea. After June, tropical hurricanes blow from 50 to 125 miles per hour. In short, the consensus was that any attempt would fail.

It was incredible. So much had been said about the difficulty of Pacific crossings by raft. From what the experts told me, it was relatively easy if one got out far enough into the westward-flowing currents. The difficulty lay in taking a route north along the coast. It was a cardinal rule for modern rafts to leave from southerly ports, preferably Callao, and to be towed out to sea until well into the westward-moving current. I expected to depart from Salaverry, 250 miles to the north. Several attempts by raft from northern ports had failed. One raft in particular, an ill-fated balsa-wood type, was caught in the doldrums near the Galápagos for more than a month and would have been doomed had a passing ship not heard its distress signals by radio and come to its aid. Though the general concern over my fate was understandable, my mind was made up. I would make use of the favorable trade winds and stay within the strongest part of the current, a branch of the Humboldt flowing north along the coast all the way to Panama Bay.

I was used to having my ideas questioned. Five years before, research into old manuscripts had convinced me that the ruins of Machu Picchu, discovered in 1911 by Yale University professor Hiram Bingham, did not answer the description of the legendary lost city of the Incas. Spanish soldiers who conquered and then abandoned the old city in the name of King Philip of Spain had declared that the city was located farther along in the steaming jungles. Specialists who were supposed to know assured me that the Incas never settled the tropics in force and that this could not be the site of the fabled lost city. Yet, on the strength of what the conquistadors had to say, I took the route they followed and reclaimed a vast metropolis in precisely the place they had reported it to be. Later, most experts agreed that it was the old city used as a refuge by the Inca kings. It was Vilcabamba.

I suppose it appeared strange to my friends and colleagues that I would want to put off my ethnological investigations simply to undertake a sea expedition. I had worked long and hard over the years to demonstrate that the forests of the upper Amazon had been the home (and grave) of many ancient peoples in Peru. Moreover, they argued, my discoveries east of the Andes were contributing to our knowledge of intercultural contacts, while a sea voyage would prove nothing. Now that my work was bearing fruit, my new project seemed like a complete turnabout. Goodness knows there were more unreported cities still out there—as I was to show later on. Some claimed that such a project might damage the reputation I had managed to build up, especially if it failed.

I didn't agree, couldn't agree. The whole idea of the expedition was the outgrowth of years of research—an extension of all my work in the interior—and I was eager to begin.

Exploring a Lost World

Using old Spanish manuscripts as a guide, I had journeyed through Amazonas in eastern Peru, 600 miles as the crow flies, north of Vilcabamba. Inca Túpac Yupanqui and his son Huayna Capac, both powerful kings in ancient Peru, reported having conquered a highly advanced civilization of white Indians called the Chachas, who occupied what was known as the Kingdom of Chachapoyas, some time between A.D. 1480 and 1511. On the strength of what the Spaniards had taken down from the oral traditions of the Incas, I set out to uncover a string of white stone cities situated on the forested heights of the Andes, along with many agricultural settlements located in the lower jungles. No one had dared imagine that so many magnificent monuments existed in the high and low jungles of eastern Peru: whole cities with bridges, fountains, temples, canals, and agricultural terracing near good water sources—all just sitting there, waiting to be explored. I had long suspected that ancient high civilizations had inhabited the jungles and that they had developed in the lower Amazon basin. But there was more to it than that.

According to the Incas, the Chachas were fair-skinned. They were popularly known as the "cloud people" because of their white skin and blue eyes. The women were very beautiful; they became the favorites of the Incas—and later were sought after by the Spaniards. Legend says that the Chacha stonemasons worked stone as expertly as did the men of Cuzco, capital city and heart of the Inca empire. I later saw evidence of their stonework. Nowhere in Peru does one find the traces of ancient peoples in such abundance. I reported over forty major sites: city layouts, ceremonial centers, temples, and agricultural settlements. There were hundreds of square miles of stone buildings embellished with geometric mosaics unlike anything previously found in Peru.

I was particularly interested in the architecture. The majority of the edifices I found were circular. In Mexico the circular buildings were sacred; they were dedicated to Quetzalcoatl. Machu Picchu, which some claim was dedicated to Viracocha, the Sun God, contains a semicircular palace. Except for the Sun Temple in Cuzco, round buildings were rare; the Incas seemed to prefer straight lines, at least in the highlands. This palace suggests that Machu Picchu must have been very sacred indeed. It also suggests a link with the Amazon, where circular buildings are the rule.

There was an unmistakable relationship among the different cultures known under so many different names that made up ancient America. One could see it in the art styles: textile weavings, ceramic pottery designs, architectural ornamentation. Both coastal and highland cultures showed an Amazonian link. A temple façade 12,500 feet above sea level would display the same designs as a skin tattoo of a lowland jungle native living but a few hundred miles from the Atlantic. The Amazonians were an organized people as far back as 3000 B.C., possibly earlier. Archaeological evidence suggests that centuries ago peoples from the tropical forests swept up from the lowlands to lay claim to the uplands, much of which appears to have been unoccupied at the time. I had traced many valley roads leading up from the jungles to the highlands. Certainly the Andes offered no barrier to ancient people. I was able to see this without benefit of excavations.

One day in late August 1965, tired from a hard climb, I sat looking at a clump of steaming vegetation which later proved to be a building. Our expedition had started from the coast and worked its way up over the Andes and down into the jungles. I put thirteen Indian machete men to work clearing away the thick vegetation. Hours later the first circular building of a temple layout came to light. Thousands of individual stone elements had been placed together like a mosaic to form the principal walls. There were step and zigzag motifs, common designs used by Amazon peoples. The site was one of several subsequent ruins reclaimed from the high forests that averaged about 9,500 feet above sea level on the slopes of the eastern Andes. There were serpentine or solar-ray decorations, representations of the coatl serpent design I had seen in Mexican architecture and symbolic of Quetzalcoatl, the Feathered Serpent. I was amazed that the same idea had been incorporated into Peruvian architecture. I put my memory to work.

Months earlier, while exploring to the west, I had had the good fortune to uncover a stone monolith that weighed over a

ton and measured nearly nine feet long. It was of black basalt
rock with two double-headed serpents—strikingly similar to
the Plumed Serpent god of the Maya, Kukulcan—incised on
its surface. The snake's body was decorated with solar and
feather designs. Rattles tipped the tails. The heads were those
of a dog (Quetzalcoatl assumed this form before entering the
Land of the Dead) with tears streaming out of its eyes. Here
was the weeping-god concept of Tiahuanaco, a depiction of
Viracocha, the Sun God. From each trumpet-shaped mouth
protruded a tongue, symbolizing wind. I chipped off flakes of
red and white paint, the colors of the Feathered Serpent. It
was this find more than any other that encouraged me to cross
the Andes to explore the rain forests in search of other artifacts
which had been covered by a thick mantle of vegetation centuries old.

Now I had an actual site to study. The walls emerged from
out of the greenery as if by magic, and my eyes were struck by
the mythological decorations incorporated into the stone work:
winged figures, also with solar crowns, indicated that the
sculptured monument was a ceremonial center honoring the
sun. When I saw the figure of a beautiful bird, probably a
condor, on one of the walls I was certain this was so. An eagle
represented the sun in Aztec monuments. The same idea was
being conveyed here. Then, when I saw the aquatic signs above
the medial molding of the structures, I thought of the ideas
symbolized at the ancient city of Teotihuacán in Mexico. The
step fret designs, angular spirals, zigzags, and aquatic signs
adorning the white walls represented the terrestrial waters.
The fire or solar signs represented heaven. Here was a perfect
representation of divine duality, the Yin and Yang of Chinese
mysticism.

The fact that these buildings were placed at the top of a pyra-
midlike mountain etched with stone platforms and approached

by stairways suggested the concepts I had studied in Mexico. The whole Quetzalcoatl idea was here, but in Peruvian form. This hypothesis was confirmed months later when I began to uncover other cities to the north with the same ideas. I found cruciform designs (connected with the sun); rhomboidal fire signs (suggestive of the Aztec fire god, Xiuhtecutli), and numerous aquatic signs (similar to those of the Aztec rain god, Tlaloc, Lord over the Terrestrial Paradise); the T-shaped glyph Ik, the eye of the Mayan god of rain, Chac, which, it has been suggested, represents both rain and fertility. The aquatic signs in particular fascinated me, for they also suggested maritime contact with Mesoamerica.

Our location on a major mountain pass that bridged the coast and lower jungle was no more than 150 miles from the ocean and only 50 miles from the Huallaga River, which flows into the Amazon itself. Commerce between the coast and the Amazon basin in ancient times is an established archaeological fact. Like other Amazon peoples, the Chachas were oriented to the rivers (I later went on to find their roads leading to the tributaries of the Amazon). The fact that we found conch shells suggested that they were not strictly a forest people. Most tribes of the tropical forests were canoe people who used the rivers for trade and commerce. Undoubtedly the Chachas had developed watercraft, as did other nations of the forests. It would have been relatively easy for them to have reached the Pacific and used their knowledge of rivers for coastal navigation. Indeed, the Kingdom of Chachapoyas faced the great maritime nations of Chimú, Mochica, and Lambayeque to the west. The abundance of coastal pottery found in the area indicates a connection between the Chachas and their neighbors and suggests that trade was maintained. Many people underestimate the worth of archaeological remains in the inner jungles.

On its way to the ruins, my mule train entered the highland community of Pataz. The church bell rang, calling out the menfolk, who quickly formed a human chain across the road, refusing to let us pass until we agreed to hire them. Our chief guide, from the upland city of Huamachuco, said they were growing poppies in the lush forests below and didn't want us nosing around. When their demands turned to threats, I agreed to take them on.

I had it on good authority that in addition to their traffic in opium, they were engaged in tomb-robbing. The police commander, when issuing my papers, had hinted that my life might be in danger if I pushed on. On an earlier occasion, one of my chief porters had been found hanging by the neck in a thatched hut the very day he agreed to lead us to ruins in southern Peru, so this time I decided to play it safe.

One of the men hired in Pataz, a dark-skinned fellow with a huge wad of coca leaves in his cheek, approached me. Tugging at my coat sleeve, he urged me down the muddy slope toward a stone platform. Skirting the edge behind my guide, who sent wild orchids flying with every swath of his machete, we came to a carved object tenoned into the wall. After clearing the mud away, I was shocked to find myself looking into the kingly face of a great dignitary with a foliated nose. It was framed by two round earplugs and crowned with a headpiece decorated with two angular spirals identical to the kind painted on the forehead of images of the Mexican Quetzalcoatl.

We explored the site (which we named Gran Pajatén) until the sun threatened to abandon us. Jaguars padded right up to our tents that night. We kept them at bay with our strong flashlight beams and with blasts from our shotguns. On the third day we were forced to pull out. Later, I was able to return by helicopter, and I succeeded in spotting the tomb of the Priest-King of Gran Pajatén, caught up on a narrow ledge of the towering limestone cliffs which dominated the site. This and other sites near the old temple city remain to be studied and excavated by some enterprising specialist who is skilled in mountain climbing.

The civilization that preceded the Kingdom of Chachapoyas is a mystery. While no archaeological proof exists for its beginnings, I obtained several carbon-14 datings, the earliest being A.D. 800, which suggests there were many centuries of prior development. The ruins I was examining were a classic example of their architecture. But what of origins? Did these people have their beginning in the cradle of the Amazon basin as I suspected? The Chachas certainly were not of Andean origin. Tropical forest peoples could not have developed on the coast. Yet certain similarities with Mesoamerica exist. How was this contact achieved? And, of still greater consequence, what of the references to the Chachas' having been fair-skinned, blue-eyed people? Was this reasonable? Or was there really a Caucasoid people in Peru before the coming of the Spaniards? And what of the Mesoamerican implications?

The White Indians of Peru

Months later I examined a small stone carving of a head with Armenoid nose, mustache, and flowing beard that farmers had dug up from one of the Chachapoyas sites. It was remarkable for its obvious European features. When I first saw it I immediately thought of the Mexican Quetzalcoatl or the Mayan Kukulcan, both of whom were reported to be white-skinned. The presence of a supposed Aryan type in the Americas has given rise to theories of pre-Columbian landings from the Old World. Proponents of such theories believe that the New World culture was dependent on the Old World; they deny the independent development of American cultures. They discount the possibility that the racial heterogeneity of the American aborigine, the hirsute stock, may be older than that of the Mongolian.

A degree of transoceanic migration was probable, but certainly whole cultures did not cross the seas. Land-bridge theories serve only to make American aborigines dependent on the Old World. How, then, do we account for the varied ethnic types, representing practically every known human race, that existed in the Americas at the time of the conquest? This fact has led the superficial-minded to speculate on contact by sea between the New World and Europe on the Atlantic side, and between the New World and Asia on the Pacific side. The Negroid cast to the giant stone Olmec heads in Mexico indicates a possible African contact. Heyerdahl suggested that the Olmecs were Nordic adventurers from across the sea. Later archaeological excavations proved that they were American Indians, however, showing again that these early Americans evolved independently. America was inhabited by yellow-, black-, and white-skinned peoples, in addition to red and brown. Many of the Caribbean peoples were lighter-skinned than the Portuguese explorers who first saw them. The Spaniards reported that the natives of Panama, the Tairones of Colombia, and the natives of the Bolivian altiplano sported better beards than theirs. The same thing was observed in the lower Amazon and among the Chachapoyas of Peru. This shows that the unity of races is not an established fact and that thinking of the Americans as one type is as absurd as speaking of "typical" Caucasians. The light-skinned Chachapoyas of Peru do not suggest a sea landing any more than does the presence of the Ainus in northern Japan. Americans were simply here, possibly before the continents began to drift apart.

It is quite possible that sea trade in ancient times linked the various cultures, but this came at a relatively late date. The origin of American man is quite another story.

If I could establish that Chacha people were really white, it would be the first actual proof that such a people existed in Peru. Artistic representations alone are really not reliable anthropological proof. I would need more than carvings.

I began to reconnoiter the forests of Amazonas for evidence, spending as much as five months at a time in the jungle. One day, while walking down a trail, I was startled to see coming out of the jungle five tall, blue-eyed men with long blond hair. Farther along I met and conversed with another man who was at least six feet five inches tall. This giant was as blue-eyed as I am, white-skinned, with dirty blond hair. The Italian explorer Raimondi had reported seeing the skeleton of an ancient Chachapoyan seven feet tall. Here was corroboration of his find. As I came into a village, my eyes worked like movie cameras as they recorded things I hadn't expected to see: Among the children playing in the plaza, typically dark-skinned, were many who were fair, blue-eyed or green-eyed, with blond hair; the upper hills were lined with white stone buildings jutting out of the forests; village women wrapped in blue and white shawls were negotiating stone stairways and balancing clay jugs on their heads; stone figures of the sage-king I had seen at Pajatén protruded from the mud and rock walls of the houses; condors were soaring overhead in the royal Andean blue skies; clear water was splashing from old fountains, sparkling in the sun and filling the air with a tranquilizing sound. So it went, from village to village, living evidence that white men had occupied and are still occupying the area.

Everywhere I went the people talked of an ancient learned man who, like themselves, was fair-skinned. He had lived centuries earlier and had taught the people the civilized arts and the sciences of a new religion.

The village elders of Shipasbamba did in fact show me an old manuscript, No. 109 of the municipal archives, written A.D. 1597 by Juan de la Cruz Aguilar, a local judge, which mentioned an ancient holy man who was bearded and in other aspects resembled the legendary Viracocha of the Incas of southern Peru. Catholic friars at Chachapoyas identified him with Saint Thomas, who had come to the Indies to teach the Christian message, not suspecting that aborigines would be able to produce a holy man of their own. The manuscript mentioned an ancient community of circular buildings called Tiapollo or Villunca that was dedicated to him (which backed up my own theory that Gran Pajatén, among many other Chachapoyan cities, was a monument to a great dignitary who had lived in former times). The old work refers to a mythological coiled feathered serpent (Puru Solpe Machaco) that lived in subterranean places, especially caves; the wandering prophet was related to this serpent. Eventually he disappeared into the western ocean.

Mythology of American Culture Heroes

Perhaps the most noted of all Peruvian mythological figures that have come down to us is Con Ticci Viracocha. The name may be translated as "God, Creator of the World"; some sources say it meant "the unknowable god." The chronicles of Pedro de Cieza de León, among a number of other sources, tell us the name meant "sea foam." Other early writers denied this, saying the name meant "man from the sea," or "god from the sea."

According to legend, long before the time of the Incas, a period of great suffering came to the Peruvians. The sun did not shine for a long time. Then from the regions of the south there appeared a white man of large stature, clothed in a white robe belted at the waist. He had long hair and a flowing white beard. He became known as a world teacher and was often identified with the Creator. He commanded great respect among the people. He was depicted with a staff in one hand and a book in the other. He was accompanied in his wandering by two assistants, a fox and a lion. He traversed all the land, working miracles and healing the sick; by his words alone the blind were made to see. The people erected temples to him and carved statues in his likeness. He instituted a religion of the sun, instructing his people to live properly, to do no harm to anything, and to love and be charitable to one another. From the city of Tiahuanaco he sent out his assistants, one to the coast and the other to the eastern rain forests, to teach his religion. Then, assuming the guise of an old man, he journeyed to Cacha. There the people stoned him. Eventually he took the highland road to the north and, having reached the edge of the sea, went on to Manta, Ecuador, where he bade farewell to his people, walking out onto the waters of the Pacific with his company as naturally as he had traversed the land. Legend says that at a later date his two sons, Imaymana and Tocapo, appeared walking the highland and lowland roads to all the world to preach and restore the doctrines of Viracocha. The first, when he reached the sea, ascended into the sky. The other, putting his mantle into the water as he would a boat, went forth into the sea and disappeared.

Another cultural hero of Peru, Thunupa Viracocha, arrived in the Lake Titicaca basin from the north with five disciples. Bearded and blue-eyed and wearing a *cuchma*—a long tunic popular with jungle folk—he appeared to be a man past his prime with long gray hair. He carried a large wooden cross on his back and walked with a staff. He had the gift of tongues and preached from a book. His was a mission of love and peace; many miracles were performed. But his preaching annoyed the populace, and he was forced to flee. He escaped on Lake Titicaca in a boat made of totora rush. Eventually he made his way via a river to the sea.

We find similar legends on the coast which tell of a world teacher called Con who came from the north (though some early writers say it was from the south) and taught a philosophy of the sun. Perhaps this divine figure later was merged with the historical figure known as King Naylamp. Arriving on a fleet of reed ships equipped with sails, he appeared off the coast of Lambayeque and anchored at the mouth of the Lambayeque River near the Mochica empire (some writers think it the Chancay farther to the south). He was accompanied by his subjects and by his wife, Ceterni, his harem, his children, and a court numbering forty. One of his heralds blew on a marine conch shell as he came ashore to found a city called Chot, and in his temple it was taught that the human race originated from the stars. When he died, his followers were told that he had come on wings out of the sky, and now had flown away.

I saw in this a parallel with the Gran Pajatén ruins, where the principal figures were winged, depicting flight from the earth to heaven. That these ruins had been dedicated to the culture hero Con Ticci Viracocha was apparent to me.

I had discussed the meaning of Viracocha with my good friend, the scientist Federico Kauffman Doig, who said it was a corruption of the old Quechua words *virac*, or *huillac*, and *ocha*, or *ucha*, which, literally translated, meant sacred or brilliant sacrifice.

This translation brought to mind the legends of El Dorado, the Gilded One. When the conquistadors began their explorations of the New World, they heard rumors of a mysterious people to the south governed by a priest-king. This and other rumors prompted the Spaniard Francisco Pizarro to sail to Panama; later he conquered the Inca empire. First, in the mountain regions of Santa Fé de Bogotá, they searched the Chibcha nation for a lake called Guatavita where a lord and sovereign of a nation of white Indians was known to perform a sacred ceremony on certain days of the year, probably at the winter and summer solstices. It was said that he boarded a raft and was rowed to the center of the lake, where his attendants covered him with gold dust. Praying to the setting sun, gleaming like a golden god, attired in magnificent feathers and jewels, he dived into the waters in a shower of sparkling light, offering himself as a sacrifice to the lake goddess, who assumed the form of a serpent. But each time, he was seen to emerge through the patch of flaming gold dust to rejoin his people, leaving behind a treasure as an offering.

Quetzalcoatl and the Mayan Kukulcan joined the pantheon. Quetzalcoatl landed with a large host at Veracruz. A conch shell was one of his insignia. Dressed in a long gown decorated with white crosses and wearing a feathered headdress, he came ashore, staff in hand, to instruct the populace in the arts and sciences of solar knowledge. (A myth relates that he descended in the form of a bird and assumed human shape—as depicted in the Gran Pajatén ruins.) Just as our era began with Christ, that of the ancient Mexican people began with Quetzalcoatl. He is the central and most powerful figure in the mythology of all Mesoamerica. As lawgiver, civilizer, religious teacher, and bringer of solar teachings, he exemplified a way of life superior to anything known before. Like Buddha, he was enlightened, a man who stood apart from other men. He inspired pyramid-building and gave men the calendar and a book of life explaining the solar worlds. He was tall, with a fair beard and large eyes; he wore a conical hat, a necklace of seashells, and sandals of foam. His name comes from the quetzal bird, which has brilliant green feathers, and the Nahua word for serpent and water, meaning "feathered sea serpent." It can also be translated as "precious twin," one side being Venus and the other *xolotl* or "dog." In the theology of the Mexicans, Quetzalcoatl was the Sun itself. As king of men and as god of learning, he came to offer himself as a sacrifice for the welfare of humanity in the Western Hemisphere. His cult carried new ideas that altered the lives of men over a wide area. Above all, his followers were merchants who encouraged trade. Coastal towns were used as centers of export, as in Peru and Ecuador. Though members of his cult were wealthy, they acted humbly, never accumulating personal riches, but giving to the poor. They influenced kings and lords for the overall good of the people. While they belonged to a spiritual world which they called the "Land of the Sun," they regulated the material world with great efficiency wherever their influence was felt.

Quetzalcoatl opposed the religious orders of the society he came into, preaching against war and human sacrifice. Eventually he was persecuted by the old priesthood. Destroying all his earthly possessions and throwing his treasure and jewels into the waters, he set off with his loyal disciples to climb the snowy volcanic peaks. Having reached the coast, he departed on a raft of serpents, never to return.

Where did Quetzalcoatl go after he left Mexico? If we accept the metaphysical symbolism, he set out for Anahuac, the "place at the center, in the midst of the circle." Which is to say he transcended human existence to unite with the source of all form and being. According to tradition, he sailed away to the east into the Gulf Stream, where he probably became known to the Maya as Kukulcan, or possibly Gucumatz.

The Maya had still another name for this wandering prophet. It was Votán. Votán had journeyed from the mythical land of Valum Chivím with his wife Ixchél, the rainbow—also called the spider's web catching the morning dew—to spread his teachings throughout the Maya territory.

The Quetzalcoatl-Kukulcan-Votán of Mesoamerica and the Viracocha-Bochica–El Dorado of South America have obvious connections. That these names refer to the same person or deity appears certain—though many individuals, both priests and kings, assumed the names in carrying on the tradition. The mythological traditions date from the early formations of the Chavín of Peru and the Olmec of Mexico, possibly as early as 2000 B.C. or even earlier. Historically, there appears to have been a resurgence of this body of legend throughout America beginning sometime in the first century of our era and lasting for a thousand years; it flowered when the Tiahuanaco, Mochica, Chachapoyas, Maya, and Toltecs were experiencing a legendary golden period, followed by the Incas, Chimú, Aztecs, and Chibchas, among other peoples. That so many different cultures, over such a widespread area, could share the same mythological savior demonstrates that the ideas he promoted were ingrained very deeply in the hearts of many peoples.

There is no doubt that a real flesh-and-blood teacher of great importance lived at one time. Was the kingdom of the Chachapoyas—or its forerunner—the Valum Chivím of Quetzalcoatl-Kukulcan-Votán? The only evidence of an advanced civilization of white men is that of the Chachas. Since the wandering prophet was white, it seems probable that he originated from a people fair-skinned like himself. This was a far more realistic idea than that of his making a transoceanic crossing, arriving in the New World from Phoenicia, Ireland, Greece, Egypt, Japan, or China, as some have theorized, or equating him with Christ.

I first began to suspect sea communication between Peru and Mexico when in 1961 I observed a petroglyph etched on a rock in the Jequetepeque Valley of northern Peru. It was a Mexican hieroglyph for gold, the same one I had seen carved on a statue of the Aztec Coyolxauhqui, sister of Huitzilopochtli. At the mouth of the river, overlooking the sea, stands the ruined city of Pacatnamu with seventy pyramids. This was Chimú territory. The art forms found on ceramic pottery and woven material strangely echo Mayan motifs. The case for maritime contact between south and north is strengthened by the fact that Pacatnamu and the nearby city of Chan Chan north of the Moche Valley, where we find the Pyramids of the Sun and Moon, were both seaports.

Aboriginal Watercraft

The possibility of the maritime-connection theory's finding support in mythological sources continued to fascinate me. Archaeologists are aware of the similarity of the artifacts found in old towns up and down the Pacific coast. Seagoing trade is believed to account for this. Stone carvings found in the Manabi area of the Ecuadorian coast are, according to some, more akin to those of Mesoamerica or even Chimú of northern Peru than those of the Andes.

Coastal cruising off the American coast in pre-Spanish days is an established fact. The Colombians manufactured good dugout canoes from the ceiba tree. Francisco Pizarro's second voyage to Peru, southward from Panama, established this with certainty. The canoes of northern Ecuador were described as brightly decorated, with large bows and sterns ornamented with golden objects. They were propelled by both sails and paddles. Bartolome Ruiz, Pizarro's pilot, reported that there were plying the coast large sailing rafts equipped with masts and cotton sails and rigged as effectively as the Spanish ships. Eyewitness accounts by Spanish sailors told of rafts at Santa Elena, Puna Island, Tumbez, and Manta. These rafts were capable of carrying fifty people or more and up to thirty large casks of trade goods. They were often described as being constructed of *caña*, cane or bamboo. While other reports indicate that balsa logs were used, this seems less likely because of the lack of suitable balsa timber, which grows in the uplands and not along the coast. Among the Incas, reed was the favored material for building boats.

Watercraft could have accounted for migrations and trade in early America, as suggested by mythology and partially supported by archaeology and history. On both the Pacific and Atlantic sides, large dugouts, sailing rafts, and float-type vessels were reported. The Maya were maritime people who maintained sea communications along the entire coast from Tabasco to Panama, nearly 2,500 miles. They dominated the coastal sea and were known as the "lords of the sea." When the Toltec invaders arrived, coming along the shoreline in war canoes, the Maya went out to meet them on rafts. Later, trade goods were paddled from Veracruz to Yucatán—some 650 miles—and then transported inland by foot. Sea trade would account for the conch shells, seaweed, pearls, pottery, and other goods found at Mayan cities deep within the steaming jungle interior. The stylized Teotihuacán marine motifs in the valleys of Mexico would indicate either that the builders were a seafaring people or that trade was maintained with coastal peoples.

Great trading fleets operated between Panama and Peru. They went where they liked and were capable of extended voyages, but kept within fifteen or twenty miles of the shore. The Indians had centuries of sailing experience in their blood. But nautical technology was primitive, and they were limited to coastal and inshore travel. "Ships beat along by standing off all day with the sea breeze and laying on all night with the land wind," as William Dampier reported in 1680. They could weather squalls and storms by running up on any beach, or pulling down sail; they obtained food along the way by fishing and by hunting in the forests along the coast. They steered by the sun and by dead reckoning. At night they either drifted along with favorable currents or made landfalls. Because they knew the coast well, they were relatively safe unless they allowed themselves to get well out to sea, where prevailing winds and currents swing west some fifty to one hundred miles offshore. Of course accidents will happen, and accidental voyages to the west could well have occurred. But aboriginal watercraft, as a general rule, were not limited to drift-type or downwind voyages. Unless the current was strong enough to overcome the force of the wind, they could have pointed their craft into the rising sun and sailed toward shore until they picked up a familiar landmark. An Indian with a paddle could propel a reed boat at an amazing speed, fast enough to overcome any current.

The Case for Building a Reed Boat

Of all aboriginal watercraft, the reed boat has perhaps the longest history. Totora, a species of *Scirpus,* is a water-loving reed which has a tubular stem of great buoyancy. Ancient folk gathered it into bundles. Lashed-together hulls were formed, with both ends turned up. Spaniards reported having seen reed boats on both continents. They were common in Mexico at Lake Chapala and Lake Tlaxcala. Distribution was continuous throughout western Mexico, along the Pacific coast to California. It was and still is the predominant watercraft of the Indians. Bundles of tules and bulrushes were collected by the Indians of Pyramid Lake in Nevada and made into four lower floats topped by gunwales of cattails. The prows were curved up. These primitive means of transport were very similar to those used in Ecuador and Peru. Sizes vary from the small one-man floats called *caballitos* used by the Peruvian coastal fishermen, to the larger vessels, with thatched sails, used in the highland lakes, particularly at Lake Titicaca. Earlier floats were much larger, some capable of carrying forty passengers. On the coast the *caballitos* or "little sea horses" are mounted by skilled surfmen and paddled expertly through the breakers.

Full documentation of the reed boat's antiquity is available. One can see paintings and molds of these vessels clearly illustrated on the pottery of the Mochicas, who occupied the north coast of Peru from as early as 500 B.C.

Because reed construction had been in use since antiquity, particularly on the coast of Peru, I selected totora reeds as the building material for the raft—or balsa, as such lightweight boats are called—I planned to reconstruct from ancient sources. Reed had a historical mythological-oral tradition behind it. When old Viracocha (by this time I was calling him the "Feathered Serpent") sailed away from Peru he probably used a reed boat. From my investigations they were faster, safer, and far more comfortable than wooden rafts. Mythology suggests that the larger balsas, which resembled sea serpents in many respects, were used only by the nobility. The Mochica-Chimú balsa usually had a raised prow and stern fashioned into a serpent-dog head, after the type I had seen on the stone serpent monolith near Yaután. If I wanted to reconstruct the kind of vessel used by Viracocha-Quetzalcoatl, it would have to be built of reeds.

Vessels of totora represented on a Chimú pottery vase. Human passengers and cargo are being transported in the reed floats. A priestly figure, possibly the Peruvian Conn or Viracocha, stands on the upper deck platform of the craft to the left. Redrawn from Hermann Leicht by Bill K. Dailey.

Planning the Sea Expedition

The Expedition Takes Form

Designing the *Feathered Serpent* on paper was exciting from the start. I consulted the Spanish chroniclers for what they had to say about balsas of totora. Touring the museums at Trujillo and Lambayeque gave me plenty of ideas. I examined numerous ceramic pots, making sketches of the totora craft they illustrated. Most depicted one- and two-man balsas which had been used by ancient Mochica and Chimú fishermen off the coast for centuries. José de Acosta (1539?–1600), a Jesuit from Spain, had compiled notes on these vessels during his travels in Peru. Reading an English edition of his book, *Historia natural y moral de las Indias* (1590), I came upon one of his accounts of the balsas used by the Peruvian Indians: "They make as it were faggots of bulrushes or dry sedges well bound together, which they call balsas; having carried them upon their shoulders to the sea, they cast them in, and presently leap upon them."

Born of an Inca princess and a Spanish conquistador in Peru in 1539, shortly after the conquest, Garcilaso de la Vega later went to live in Spain, where he wrote, from notes, his famous *Royal Commentaries of the Incas*. He described the reed balsas graphically:

Along the entire coast of Peru, the Indians go fishing in little reed boats . . . and the sea being very calm, they can venture four or five leagues [15 to 20 miles] from shore in these light skiffs. The fishermen, in their reed barks, remain on their knees, using as a crude rudder a piece of bamboo split lengthwise, which thus ends naturally in the form of a shovel. They row, first on one side then on the other, so skilfully in fact, that they may attain astonishing rapidity. . . .

These tiny little barks are too unstable for them to possibly rig up a sail, but, on the other hand, they do put sails on their rafts when they go out to sea.

Excitement filled my heart as I came upon a sketch of two much larger reed balsas taken from a spouted Chimú pottery vase of the Chicama valley. Here were two identical double-decked totora vessels. The hulls were formed from bundles of reed bound by thick ropes. The upswept prows and sterns had been formed into serpent or dragon heads (the same style I had seen on the monolith at Yaután). The superstructures were thatched reed and bamboo, or so it appeared. Two priestly figures stood atop the upper decks, and between them a cargo of pottery vessels was neatly arranged. Blades or leeboards at both ends formed the steering apparatus. The boats were propelled by two legs extending from the hull, running over the sea—a typical motif in Chimú art. They looked very much like keels or daggerboards with weights, which was an important point. Mochica pottery illustrations showed the same serpent heads mounted on the bow and stern of each reed boat. One in particular depicted two priestly figures abovedeck, and pots, passengers, and gear stowed belowdeck. All the vessels shared a common characteristic: One end, possibly the stern, showed two serpent heads, as if two hulls were joined. This told me that the rafts were probably multi-hulled. I formed this opinion after seeing in the museum at Lambayeque so many pottery vases showing two totora reed floats lashed together. Experts with whom I discussed the matter agreed with me.

When I talked to the museum director at Lambayeque and asked his opinion, he told me that twin-hulled rafts of totora had been used in ancient times. He showed me other examples.

The Mochica-Chimú pottery motifs showed that contact had been maintained with the jungles to the east; possibly the earlier of these two cultures could be traced to a jungle origin. Representations of monkeys, jaguars, and large snakes, and jungle scenes of men using blowguns and the like, all tended to suggest commerce between coast and jungle. Because Amazon peoples are oriented to waterways, the acquaintance of the Mochicas with the sea and coastal navigation is understandable.

With the basic design formulated, the next step was to decide on sails. While there is no archaeological evidence for sails having been used on totora floats other than the thatched ones on Lake Titicaca, this doesn't mean they could not have been used on the coast. Totora rots quickly, in spite of the dry desert climate that has preserved textiles and other artifacts. Thus no samples of sailing totora balsas from the coast have survived. However, other sources besides archaeology indicate that sails were employed. These include mythological, historical, and traditional sources; the oral traditions, in particular, indicate that sails were adapted to balsas of totora.

Lashing more than one totora hull together would give the float good stability; the leeboards or blades pictured on the Chimú and Mochica art forms are used on modern sailing vessels for balance and were employed on aboriginal sailing rafts for steering; the wooden or bamboo decks would have easily supported a mast. These characteristics add up to a good case for thinking of the larger floats as sailing vessels. While the importance of these points may be overlooked by the archaeologist, they cannot be lost to the student of sailing craft. When I showed the sketches to professional sailors, they all agreed on this point overwhelmingly. The natives with whom I have spoken insist that sails were used—they have heard this from their fathers and grandfathers.

Weeks earlier, I had flown to Connecticut to show sketches of the balsa to Robert Harris, a leading authority on old sailing craft, and Robert Bollinger of New Jersey, who was experienced on multi-hulled sailing craft. They both agreed that the stability was good and that I should have no trouble; nevertheless, they were not sure about the seaworthiness of totora, with which they were not too familiar. But they liked what they saw and made valuable suggestions. Clinton R. Edwards, the foremost authority on aboriginal watercraft in the Americas, had sent me what he believed to be the type of sailing rig used on pre-Columbian balsawood sailing rafts of the Ecuadorian and North Peruvian coastal area (a lateen type of sail), though as a scientist he couldn't state positively whether sails had ever been used on totora floats. As a blue-water sailor of some repute, he found it a fascinating undertaking, but he was not sure that the need for, or the dramatization of, such a voyage was scientifically necessary.

Other boatmen with whom I spoke emphasized the need to build a light boat with a long waterline to assure speed. They all insisted that I make the trip in the shortest possible time. It would have been relatively simple to build such a vessel and equip it with plenty of canvas. But a sea expedition of this nature wouldn't prove very much. I was fully aware of the dangers of reconstructing an actual sea voyage on the strength of mythological sources. For this reason I wanted to find, if possible, many other sources, both archaeological and historical. I planned to make the voyage as nearly authentic as my means would allow.

It was in this attempt to duplicate primitive conditions that I encountered the most difficulties. I expected to make compromises—these couldn't be avoided. Certain materials used in olden times are no longer available. And I didn't think logistics demanded that I live on raw fish and bananas. But I didn't want to take aboard a gasoline generator for lights, radio receiver with transmitter, and other navigational aids. It wouldn't have been a fair test. If I had had my choice I would have picked a native crew for the journey. And we would have sailed by the sun and stars and dead reckoning, as aborigines did in the past.

Navigational Problems

I had studied coastal navigation as a youth and had sailed a catsailboat on the lakes of Oregon. I felt qualified to sail the totora boat up the coast with the help of a native crew. These men knew the coast well, and I had read and studied the charts from Peru to Mexico. Since we wouldn't be sailing deep sea, there was no need for a sextant or navigational equipment. However, the publicity generated by the news media set many tongues to wagging. It was said I would be carried out to Polynesia or beyond to Australia by strong westward-flowing currents. I was politely informed by the Peruvian port authorities that the craft would be under maritime law, which meant that if I failed to comply with the law, I would not be allowed to sail. It also meant that I would be required to take on a qualified and competent navigator (acceptable to the Peruvian navy), modern navigational instruments, radio receiver and transmitter, foghorn, lights, flare pistol, depth-sounding lead, anchor, food and water for the crew, and a host of other things. A battleship would be needed to carry all that gear! I was crestfallen.

I had anticipated some difficulties along these lines weeks before and had invited Dr. George O'Neill, archaeologist-anthropologist at the City College of New York, to participate in the expedition as observer. But at the last moment he was forced to withdraw because of other commitments. I did not want to take along a stranger. Some of the best people you would want to meet—really great over a cup of tea or at the theater—degenerate into sniveling, bad-tempered, hard-to-please individuals on an expedition. Perhaps it is the jungle environment, the primitive conditions, or the weather and change of habits (no hot baths, no taxis, no corner store out there). When comforts are limited to basic necessities—food, rest, and sleep—one's whole character and personality may change.

Now I would be forced to live with a stranger for weeks on end within the confines of a small deck a few feet across. I telephoned half a dozen friends. "I need help," I said. "How would you like to serve as navigator on my new expedition? Won't take more than two or three months, at the most. I am sailing from Peru to Middle America. Can't pay anything, but a great opportunity for adventure." A long wait, then the inevitable questions: "What kind of boat is it? When do you sail?"

I would cough and reply: "It's a primitive boat of totora. We sail in about two months."

Not being familiar with the Indian word, they would ask: "What is totora?"

"It's a reed. Grass," I would answer quickly.

"You mean a straw boat!"

"Well, kind of. But don't worry," I'd say. "It will float."

Then would come a long period of silence, followed by the inevitable refusal.

I tried desperately to find someone. Then one day, after I had returned to Peru to go ahead with my plans, a knock came at the door. I opened it to confront a tall, heavy-set man, with dark hair and brown eyes, in a faded brown suit.

"Remember me?" he said. Yes, I did remember. He had attended one of my photo exhibits two years before. "I read you are making the expedition." His English wasn't good but he knew his worth. I asked him to come in and sit down.

"As before, I offer my services as navigator." I had forgotten; we had talked briefly about the possibility of his going, but I had dismissed the idea when he dropped out of sight. He was Tomas Serafini, an Italian citizen residing in Peru.

"Could you really go?" I asked. "And do you have papers?"

"Yes . . . of course. I have commanded a ship in the Italian navy." With this statement he spread his arms as if I had offended him. He opened an old briefcase and proudly showed his numerous credentials. They ranged from a doctorate in naval engineering to an official paper stating that he had commanded a powered sailing vessel on a four-month cruise from Italy to the African coast to the South Atlantic.

Next day, when I saw him again, I gave him a general rundown of the requirements. I stressed the fact that he was expected to go without pay. He agreed.

"I want only to be a useful member. This is a great opportunity for me to find glory again," he stated with great fanfare. "I have won Germany's Iron Cross as a parachutist-ranger in North Africa, at the battle of El Alamein, when serving with the Italian army under General Rommel and Il Duce."

"Did you know the general personally?" I inquired.

"Oh, yes. A wonderful man. I loved the desert and learned to speak Arabic. I also speak five other languages—French, Portuguese, a smattering of Greek, German, and Swahili; and aside from my own language, Spanish and English."

This was all good; perhaps *too* good to be true. No matter. I needed a navigator and decided to take a chance. "Well," I said, putting out my hand, "serving as navigator on a reed boat won't be the same as commanding a ship of the line in the Italian navy." He took my hand and we both laughed.

The expedition was on again. I could think of nothing else.

The Old Seamen of Huanchaco

Weeks passed. Flights to New York and meetings with sponsors. A thousand things to be done in Lima. Then the time came for me to fly to Trujillo, 250 miles north of Lima, accompanied by the expedition's navigator. There I was to meet an old friend and companion from my jungle explorations. His name was Segundo Grandez. He had been my right-hand man in the interior for a number of years, and it was hard for me to think of making an expedition without him.

Thirty-five years old, short and powerfully built, Segundo Grandez was endowed with brown skin, curly hair, and a pair of quick black eyes set in an intelligent, handsome face that wore a perpetual smile. When he first came to ask me for work, in the small village of Rodriguez de Mendoza in eastern Peru, he told me he had lived in the forests for years tending his father's cattle. I liked him and gave him a job as guide. In the beginning he couldn't tell the difference between a natural rock and one made by man, but it did not take him long to learn how to root out ancient ruins like an expert. There was no better man with a machete; with a deft flick of his wrist he could cut a three-inch-thick vine as easily as most would a leaf, and never tire. It took a long time to get him used to horses. But he could pick out a small movement in the foliage that others wouldn't notice. This keen perception had served me well on a number of occasions. He used to delight in cutting away the thick vegetation to reveal stone walls and would run back like a child to make his report. He kept the men in line, and we were never short of provisions, whether fish from the nearest stream or lake, wild honey taken from a hollow tree, eggs picked from the floor of the jungle, or monkeys, a delicacy which he and the other men relished.

All folk from the jungle love the water, and Segundo was no exception. He supposed a coastal voyage wouldn't be much different from a trip on an Amazon stream. Segundo was certain he could master the totora float I intended to build, and he had agreed to accompany me on the trail of the Feathered Serpent.

The navigator and I stepped off the plane at Trujillo's small, dusty, wind-swept airstrip. I was about to hail a taxi when somebody grabbed me. It was Segundo. He gave me a bear hug and tweaked my long mustache. "*Oye*, good friend," he said, tugging at the black strands of his new beard, grown especially for the trip, "the Viracochas are gathering for the great adventure." He added, "I am a little black, but if I am good the spirits of the sea will take no notice of my color." We both laughed aloud. I introduced him to our navigator. Segundo shook his hand, eyed him up and down, then took my bags. We walked to a waiting cab and drove straight to the hotel. There we left the navigator. After putting my bags away at the small apartment I had in the city, Segundo and I headed out to Huanchaco, a fifteen-minute drive.

On the way, Segundo asked me about the navigator, and I explained why we had to take him on the expedition. He spoke in the traditional sing-song Spanish dialect of the jungle. "But, Gene," he said, "the old sailors of the coast did not have scientific instruments or navigators to use them. They knew the ocean like we of the jungle know the rivers. Like the palms of our hands." He stuck out his wide hand to emphasize his point. "I don't have faith in this stranger or his instruments. How can the voyage be authentic with a modern navigator on board?"

Before answering, I looked out the window and took in the great mud walls of the ruined city of Chan Chan; once the capital of the Chimú, it had boasted a population of anywhere from 50,000 to 250,000 before the conquest. I never tired of looking at it. As the walls faded into the distance, I turned and spoke: "We don't have any choice. It's either take him or put off the expedition." I admitted he was absolutely right and told him so. He thought for a moment before replying. "No good will come of it," he said.

Very little was said the rest of the way to Huanchaco. When we arrived, we got out and walked down to the beach. Everything was bathed in sunshine. The pounding of the waves rang in our ears. A small fishing village on the coast, Huanchaco boasts menfolk who claim to be descendants of the Mochica and Chimú. Today they still fish with the small *caballitos de totora*, much the same as was done five hundred to a thousand years before. The village is nothing more than a few mud houses thatched with totora roofs, a small plaza, and municipal buildings. A rickety wharf jetting out into the sea serves the few motorboats that are moored there. The harbor affords poor shelter and is not adaptable to modern seacraft. As we walked down to the beach, a long line of *caballitos*, some forty in all, stood upended, drying in the midmorning heat. One of the fishermen, dressed only in pants cut above the knee, golden-brown skin aglow in the sun, threw a pile of nets, hooks, and bait down on the black sand. He reached up and pulled down one of the *caballitos*, about twelve feet long and made of from fifty to sixty pounds of totora—which weighs considerably more when wet—and carefully tied his fishing gear in a small hollow near the truncated end. With its raised tip, it looked like a large Arabian slipper. Then, picking it up and holding it over his head, he trotted toward the water. Flipping it over, he jumped astride and rowed right through the breakers and headed out to sea. With luck, he would return hours later with at least thirty pounds of fresh fish.

By drying the totora daily, these fishermen maintain a serviceable boat that, with care, lasts anywhere from six weeks to two months, with a cash outlay of little more than five dollars. What I had in mind would require nearly a ton of totora—the combined weight of about forty of the one-man *caballitos*—the largest totora float to be built in these parts for several centuries.

The sky was streaked with white patches of clouds, and one could hear the wind coming from the south. It was early March and the trade winds were starting to blow. If we were going to sail we would have to hurry. "Come on," I said, throwing an arm over Segundo's shoulder. "José is expecting us." The night before, I had discussed the project of building the *Feathered Serpent* with José Arzola-Huamanchumo, born and raised in Huanchaco and a master builder of *caballitos*. He had been working with totora all his life, and I had promised to show him plans of the boat. If anybody could build such a vessel I knew it was he.

When we reached the door of his home—a small house made from thatched totora and bamboo—fifty-three-year-old José came out to greet us. He was surrounded by happy bright-eyed children, who jumped around like kangaroos. We were escorted inside to waiting coffee and parched corn. His nine children stood around the table looking at us with wide eyes, while Mama Arzola-Huamanchumo fussed over us, as every Peruvian housewife does with guests. Papa looked like a pottery figure from a Mochica vase—bronze skin; thick, powerful torso and shoulders; heavy muscular legs; large hands; dark curly hair; long head with high cheekbones; wide mouth and full lips; a nose with wide-flaring nostrils. His bright, almond-shaped eyes radiated the typical honesty and frankness of the native sailor with the inbred wisdom of the sea. Midway through the second cup of coffee I coughed to catch José's attention. Pulling out the plans for what I believed to be a reconstructed Mochica vessel, I spread them on the table for him to examine.

"Can you build such a boat?" I asked. "How much totora will

it require, and is this amount available? I must sail on or before the fifteenth of next month."

José studied the drawings carefully. I left him alone with Segundo and went outside. A film crew from CBS News was scheduled to arrive in about two weeks to begin filming. I had promised to be well into building by that time and ready to sail two weeks later. To put everyone's mind at ease (since totora from the highlands has greater buoyancy) and to save time, I had ordered four large reed floats built by the natives of Lake Titicaca. Unfortunately, when the floats arrived by truck, they were found to be rotten inside. Green totora, not sufficiently dried, had been used. Now everything depended on whether José and his helpers would take time out from their fishing to build a raft. José had laughed when he saw the floats from Titicaca. He said that highlanders were babies at making boats of totora.

"A lake is not the ocean," he said. "What do those farmers know of the sea? These floats wouldn't last twenty-four hours in the sea."

He was absolutely right. What I needed were men who knew how to make an oceangoing vessel of totora—one that would hold together. I wasn't sure that they could build such a craft. Suddenly I felt tired. The wind shifted and came from the sea. I drew several deep breaths to ease the tension in my stomach. After a few minutes I went back inside. I sat down and said, "José, can you build such a float?"

He gazed into my eyes for a long time before answering. "Here is the kind of boat my ancestors sailed," he said, tapping the sketch with the back of his fingers. "I have seen these boats in my dreams."

"Will you build it for me?"

"It presents no problems. It is nothing more than a large *caballito* with platform and sailing rig."

"Do you know anything about sailing ships?"

"Señor Savoy, I am an old Huanchaquero [man from Huanchaco]. We have always used sails on our *caballitos de totora*." He told me how the fishermen adapt sails to their little boats when fishing far out, how they use paddles as rudder and keel. He was most emphatic about his ancestors having used sails on their floats of totora.

"But there is no scientific evidence that sails were ever used on totora boats," I said casually.

"I do not care what the scientists choose to believe. The evidence is here." He gave his chest a blow with his fist. "My father taught me how to sail, and his father before him. It has been so for thousands of years."

"Is there enough totora for such a boat?"

"The totora belongs to the community. But I will speak with the city council myself."

"If there is enough, could you build the float before April fifteenth?"

"If I can find enough helpers. I will speak to my uncle and to my nephew. And to my son. They will all help."

"How many men will you require?"

"A dozen should be enough." He turned his eyes back to the sketch. "I will build you a larger boat than this. The floats from Titicaca were too short." They had measured 21½ feet in length. He thought a moment. "Yes, we will build them eleven meters long [a little more than 36 feet]."

He continued to make calculations. I made some of my own. With a larger set of floats we would have more room to move about (a deck can get awfully small after a few weeks at sea). I would also require more materials. However, I did not intend to argue with José. I wanted him to use his own judgment as much as possible, just so long as he followed the basic form. I had hoped to keep it light—light enough for three or four men to manhandle on the beach, if necessary. But as we got down to figures, I estimated that the raft would be double the size of our original estimate: from one metric ton to something like two tons. We would need a larger crew. An hour passed. Finally we agreed on wages for him and for each of the other men. He promised to give me his decision the next day.

As we were leaving, José turned to Segundo and said, "We must build this boat." His voice was filled with excitement, and he accepted it as a real challenge. It would also make him a hero in the community. He was intelligent enough to realize this. And he would earn three times what he could make fishing.

Later, Segundo and I caught a cab for Trujillo.

Once we were out of sight, Segundo danced a little jig, then dug an elbow into my ribs. "He will build the float." That night I went to bed a little hungry, as I had so many nights before. For several weeks now I had found it increasingly diffi-cult to swallow my food. The past few days it had been all but impossible to eat anything; I couldn't even take liquid. It would go down just so far, then come up again. "What is the reason?" I kept asking myself. Was I tense from worry and strain from all the years of exploring? My doctor had forbidden the ex-pedition and urged me to return to the States for a complete checkup. He wouldn't tell me what was the matter, and his eyes gave me no encouragement. And with the mention of the Mayo Clinic, I could think of only one thing. If I was seriously ill, I thought, it would be better to finish my career at sea, on expedition. I could think of nothing worse than spending the last days of my life in a hospital with white walls and indif-ferent nurses. On this point I was stubborn. I felt no fear—only a deep disappointment that fate might deny me my life's ambi-tion.

When faced with the possibility of death, the mind conjures

up crazy notions. It could be any one of a number of diseases prevalent in the Amazon forests. Once when my foot had become infected, I thought I had *pie de madera*, a fungus that attacks the circulation of the leg; it enters the soles of the feet, like hookworm, from going barefooted. I had once seen a man with his swollen leg, raw and bleeding, swung up in a crooked arch over his shoulder, as if frozen permanently in that position from kicking a football. Amputation is the only cure. Of course I didn't have that ailment. But what did I have? As I lay in the darkness, alone, my mind began to wander. Finally it took flight into the past, and I was in the jungle again. . . .

The Curse of Purun Machu

Segundo is cooking oatmeal over an open fire. The men are up and someone has been sent out to round up the mules and horses. I slip out of my sleeping bag and sit on the edge of my cot. One of the men brings me a cup of hot chocolate braced with raw suger. Smoke, looking for an escape from the tiny room, curls toward the thatched roof. My eyes burn. A mule bolts past the door, refusing to take the saddle. I don't blame him; there is a large open sore on his back. I drink the thick liquid and put the cup on the dirt floor. Pulling on my pants and boots, I go outside and look at the sun. It is a beautiful day; not a cloud in the sky. We are 11,000 feet above sea level. One can see for miles—as clean as the first day of creation. I think of New York executives who look out the window of their sixty-story office buildings at the smog and think the whole world is polluted. How vast it is! Factories and cities are but small dots on the face of the earth.

I walk down a hill to wash in the small stream that flows quietly below the Indian hut, where the expedition has put up for the night. The air is rich with the aroma of wildflowers. Bees flit from blossom to blossom. Butterflies as big as my hand waft by. I wash my face and brush my teeth. The water feels wonderfully refreshing. Then I walk back up the hill and eat breakfast. I drink three cups of freshly ground coffee, then go back inside to roll up my sleeping bag and pack my gear. Today we will climb the face of the great cliff over the ruins to inspect the tombs of ancient kings. I'll need my ropes and climbing equipment. The metal pitons feel cool to the touch. The nylon rope is stiff. I place a pair of leather gloves in my belt along with a woolen, Indian *chullo* for my head. A hat will do no good. I need my machete for the jungle growth and wild grass. I buckle it on and go outside. A dozen men are waiting. Three saddle animals will take Segundo, myself, and our muleteer up the forested hill to the top of the great limestone cliff. From that point we will descend over treacherous loose-hanging rocks to the tombs.

It is an hour later and we are there. The sun is hot and we are all sweating. Coming out on a ledge, we tie a rope around a tree and throw it over the cliff. Slowly we descend—one at a time. Finally we reach a cave filled with thousands of skeletons. Beyond that we come to a ledge a thousand feet above the valley floor. Just beyond, a series of rock tombs cemented with mud and painted with geometric designs jut out into the empty sky. How the ancients ever managed to put them there I will never know. The men will not go inside the tombs. They are afraid. They nervously sniff vinegar up their noses and stuff wads of coca leaves into their mouths, then follow them with dabs of quicklime to reduce the alkalinity. This is to ward off the spirits of Purun Machu, an old man who haunts the high places and causes all manner of afflictions, the most prevalent being one in which the victim spits foam and cannot eat.

Then there is Puru Solpe Machaco, a seven-headed feathered serpent that lies coiled in the caves and tunnels, waiting to strike the unsuspecting who venture into its lair. Also the danger of "antimonia," the supposed disease of spitting blood caused by deleterious emanations from the excavations of old tombs and cemeteries. All are part of the traditional folklore of the people of Peru. Old Purun Machu, the devil-spirit, was a living force in the vicinity of ancient remains. Anyone who doubted his existence was a fool, or so the men said. I had always been warned by the natives not to enter the tombs or tunnels that disappeared into the depths of the earth. None would ever accompany me, so I went alone. They would wait outside for my return, always showing utter amazement when I appeared into the sunlight again. Today they warn me again and refuse to go with me.

I reach the caves and sit down. Huge condors soar across the face of the opening. Slowly they gather in ever-increasing numbers. Then they swoop down at me like fighter planes. I am in their nesting grounds. I am an intruder. The giant birds lay their eggs on the soft floor of the dusty caves. The Chachapoyas Indians placed the remains of their dead kings and priests in these very same caves. All around are stacks of mummies wrapped in leather skins and nets of knotted cord. The Chachas were a cave-dwelling sect, and caves played an important part in their religious life as extensions of mythological beliefs. It is no coincidence that large egglike stones are found in the vicinity of their ruins. They were worshiped as sacred objects. The primary life force was believed to be enclosed within a spherical form, the egg being the cause of creation. Like the Incas, the Chachas believed that man originated from caves. The condor was the patron of the bird cult. Its image is found represented on temple walls and tombs alike. From earliest times the messengers of the gods assumed the forms of birds. Small wonder that caves and subterranean passages play an important part in the folklore of modern Indians.

But I am an old spelunker from years past. Caves and tunnels fascinate me. I never miss an opportunity to explore one.

I decide to explore for a while, then climb down to the men. I can see by their faces that I might just as well be someone returning from the dead. They will not come near me. The particular tunnel I chose to examine was believed by the locals to contain two men frozen in solid rock for having entered ages ago. (I did in fact find two stalagmites that appeared, from a distance, to resemble human forms.) The chief of the village, who was kind enough to allow his men to accompany us, shakes his head. He tells his men that I am under the ancient curse of Purun Machu. I tell him that I do not believe in the curse, though I do respect the tombs of the ancients and for this reason never excavate or disturb them—a fact which always makes the natives respect me. (It was for this reason, more than any other, that the men were encouraged to work for me.) When I explain that the figures inside are nothing but stone, it only fortifies their belief in the legend. The men talk in hushed tones and stare silently at the myriads of bats now coming out of the mouth of the cave with a wild beating of wings. Then the men slip away into the jungle, leaving me alone with Segundo. Shortly after this I begin to spit foam and experience difficulty in swallowing.

Then I fall asleep. I sleep for some time; dreams come and go. I remember one vivid dream in particular. Entering an underground passageway, I walked for hours through damp rocks only to come out into an underground city filled with magnificent statues of black marble. I came to a door and entered a room filled with golden objects. I struck a match. The room lit up in a fantastic array of sparkling jewels. Then the light faded.

I open my eyes to find the sunlight coming in through the window of my room. I lie there for several minutes reliving the scene. Then the sound of knocking comes to my ears. It is Segundo.

"Gene," comes his voice, "it is seven o'clock."

"All right, I am coming. Meet me at the car." I shave and hurriedly shower. The splashing water evokes another dream I have often had whenever troubled, even since childhood. It involves a giant wave that slowly swells before my eyes into a towering column of water. Slowly it rolls toward me. I seem to be on a small island—or boat. Absolutely helpless, I stand frozen, watching it reach a crest, then fall sickeningly upon me. Helpless to flee or to resist, I wait for the impact, only to awaken in a cold sweat before it strikes. So it is tonight. Whenever I look at the sea, I remember this dream. There is no logical explanation for it. I have never been afraid of the sea. When a hurricane struck an aircraft carrier on which I was training, I found it invigorating; as a sea scout I loved handling a sailboat in stormy seas—and did it well. But there is some indefinable challenge about this expedition. I can't place my finger on it. Maybe I have to prove something to myself. What that something is I do not presume to know.

Pottery design from Chicama Valley, Peru, depicting two multi-hulled boats made of reeds and lashed with cord. The lower deck is lined with pots. The upper deck, supporting a priestly figure—possibly the coastal Conn, often identified with Viracocha—was probably made of bamboo cane. Rudder oars and centerboards in the shape of human legs suggest that vessels were equipped with sails, though sails are not shown. These and other ceramic representations were models that helped the author design the Feathered Serpent. *Redrawn by Bill K. Dailey from a drawing in Hermann Leicht's* Pre-Inca Art and Culture, *the clay vessel is from the collection in the Museum für Völkerkunde, Munich, West Germany.*

———◄━►———

Building the *Feathered Serpent*

At the Pyramids

It was decided by José and his men to build the *Feathered Serpent* at Huanchaco. Our boatyard was an empty lot around the corner from José's home. Fenced in and private, it was ideal for construction purposes. Curious villagers were perched on the surrounding rooftops, eager to observe for themselves the building program they had heard so much about. Talk had spread fast that I had ordered some 120,000 Peruvian soles' worth of building material—a good deal more than many of them would earn from fishing over the next ten years.

The city council agreed to provide us with all the totora we needed. José had taken me out to the pits, north of the village, where the reeds are grown. Totora requires about nine months to mature. There simply wasn't enough. So we drove out to the ruined city of Chan Chan in search of ripe totora. The once-great city of Chan Chan covers about twenty square miles. It was the largest pre-Columbian port city of South America. The forty-foot walls of the many enclosed squares are made of *tapia*—bricks of adobe, rock, and potsherds. The city once boasted temples, pyramids, houses, courtyards, and gardens.

Totora was—and still is—grown in sunken stone-lined reservoirs or *pozos.*

When we went down to examine the totora, the reeds were found to be green; local fishermen had gotten there before us and cut the ripe totora.

José wasn't discouraged. He had friends in Moche. So we took a dusty road out to the Pyramids of the Sun and Moon. Like Chan Chan, the ruins were near the sea. The remains of an old port are still to be seen. The area has been inhabited continuously for 3,000 years or more. The Mochicas had built the largest single structures on the whole Peruvian coast. The Pyramid of the Sun measures 450 by 75 feet and is approached by a ramp 290 feet long. It stood 145 feet high and was made from millions of sun-dried adobe bricks covered by liquid mud and painted over in bright colors. Investigations have shown that a mixture of lime and seashells was used in the paint, giving the surface a bright or iridescent glow, especially at night under a full moon. The Pyramid of the Moon, located on the wind-swept desert across from the Pyramid of the Sun, is smaller. Excavations have shown that it was once richly decorated with architectural ornamentations in seven colors. These designs are gone now, having been defaced by tomb-robbers and worn away by the abrasive action of wind and sand. Torrential rains that visit the deserts every fifty years take a further toll on these magnificent remains.

Some aspects of life have changed little over the centuries here. Farmers still press sun-dried adobe bricks and grow totora reeds as in ancient times. We watched the men cutting the stalks just above the surface of the ground with their machetes. José explained that cutting in this way leaves a short root which will grow again, producing ripe totora in six to nine months. A dozen cuttings are possible before a new planting is necessary. Cutting and planting are continuous throughout the year and have been for several decades. Cutting rights are administered by the village authorities—a tradition that goes back to ancient times when priesthood hierarchies controlled the cultivation of totora to assure a regular supply. Virgins from the Temples of the Sun and Moon were in charge of drying it. It was also used as a food source in ancient times. "Totora has always been a very special crop to us," said José, "and, like a woman, great care must be given to it."

The men of Moche were kind and understanding. Their eyes flashed when they heard we were to build and sail a Mochica-type boat north to Central America or maybe even to Mexico. They agreed to sell us matured totora at standard prices. Runners dispatched the word, and the collection of the highest grade of totora reed measuring three, preferably four, yards in length began. José had ordered twenty-eight *cargas* (bundles) for immediate delivery. With the dozen or so *cargas* from Huanchaco we would have some two thousand pounds—more than the village of Moche used in an entire year.

Overjoyed at our good fortune, we walked along the dusty path that ran parallel to an irrigation canal. At the Pyramid of the Sun we decided to climb to the top. Making our way to the summit over broken mud bricks, we sat down to take in the view. A cool breeze from the ocean rippled the green sea of rice and sugar cane spread out below. Neither of us said anything. But the wind seemed to speak for us. It spoke of Mochica sons now harvesting the sacred totora for a great ship to be built as their fathers had, ten thousand, nay, twenty thousand moons ago. It told of the noble fleets that sailed these same waters carrying rich cargo for trade with their brothers to the north, and of noble Viracocha, who had sailed away on such a ship, emerging as Quetzalcoatl to the Mexicans. The trees heard and whispered the message to the grass. All living things were conscious of the new activity; they knew that this

Valley of the Kings was continuing a tradition that had been sleeping.

Construction Begins

Next day, José and I got to the business of hiring men. Rolling up our sleeves to quartermast, we sat at a table made from a crooked piece of wood thrown over a pair of sawhorses and opened the workbook. There was a good number of available native shipwrights. We had decided to hire ten men in addition to José's eighteen-year-old son Abilio, an expert in *caballito*-surfing and an apprentice at totora construction. Abilio wanted to help his father build what he called "the grandfather of all *caballitos*." A nephew of José, Mercedo Huamanchumo, was the first to sign on. Twenty-four years of age, also an expert at *caballitos*, he, like Abilio, was excited at the prospect of participating, and after putting his name in the book, he pranced proudly back and forth in full view of the long lines of spectators who had come down to watch the proceedings. The other men who signed on were all older, like José's brother, a man of sixty-three whom we simply called Azcona. I would be dependent on these older hands at carpentry and totora binding.

I had my eye on the younger Mercedo and Abilio. I knew that the older men could not be induced to venture much beyond the old fishing grounds. Though they had traveled the coast as far south as Lima and up to the Ecuadorian frontier, these trips had been made in earlier days when the men were much younger. Abilio's and Mercedo's hearts pounded with the enthusiasm of youth. They knew the coast as far north as Paita —and I could predict that they would learn the rest of the way from local fishermen. This knowledge would give the ex-

pedition a better chance of success during the first critical days
at sea.

Reporting for duty, the navigator pulled up in a taxi. He was
carrying the expedition's sextant. Immediately he was dubbed
"El Navegante" or "El Ingeniero," and that is what we called
him thereafter. The shipwrights looked at the tall figure, winked
at one another, and laughed to themselves. I heard one say
that the instrument would make good weight for fishing lines.
Another one joked that the "gringo" would find out how old
Peruvians sailed the seas in balsas, if he didn't stick one of his
big feet through the totora. Nothing personal was intended
against the navigator; the Mochica shipwrights were just having
clean fun, since they believed instruments for navigational purposes were superfluous. But, weeks later, when construction
on the balsa was nearing completion, El Navegante suggested
to José that outriggers be attached to the twin floats as a precaution against capsizing. José nearly dropped his measuring
tape when he heard these words; then he laughed, saying that
the balsa was multi-hulled and would be safe as she was.

"I am not overly optimistic," said the navigator; "it may
sink." The men had toiled lovingly over the *Feathered Serpent*,
doing their best to duplicate the architectural efforts of the
old Mochica boat builders. The mere mention that she was
unseaworthy or might capsize was an insult, not only to themselves but to the ancient tradition they represented. José turned
fiercely on the navigator; then, holding himself in check, he
said, "All will go well where Señor Savoy goes, Ingeniero."
After that the navigator was held suspect among the Huanchaqueros.

Totora had started to arrive just after sunrise. The long reeds
were bound in *cargas* weighing forty to fifty pounds each.
The larger bundles were composed of roughly twenty-three

puñadas (fistfuls), as they are called. Each *carga* contained about 2,500 individual reeds. Each stem had been dried in the sun, and no curing of any kind was done. Each one was carefully inspected and placed by hand in the huge floats—over 100,000 in all were used. It was this personal and expert attention to every detail while building the balsa that would permit her to weather the storms, heavy seas, and hardships to come. I can well understand the resentment felt by José, and shared by the other men, at the navigator's lack of confidence in their work. The older men from Huanchaco resented any modern sailor and his ships made of steel or wood and driven by gasoline or diesel engines. Perhaps this explains why no one was allowed to do much more than observe their work. They had studied my plans carefully and knew what I wanted. Although they discussed with me the work from day to day, I left them pretty much on their own.

Even Segundo learned to keep out of their way. Once when he pointed out what he thought to be a mistake, he was told politely but firmly that jungle men knew nothing of the sea. Segundo had replied that dugouts and balsa rafts were used in the interior and that the tributaries of the Amazon weren't so small. He described whirlpools that often took big wooden rafts laden with bananas to the bottom, of big rapids and the dangers of piranha. "Wait 'til the land fades from sight and the sea comes pounding down on you. Wait 'til you feel the wind tearing at your flesh. As for piranhas, what are they to sharks?" Segundo shrugged his shoulders and went on with his own work, muttering something to himself that sounded like he "would soon enough show them whether a Chachapoyano could take what the sea had to offer or not." As for the navigator, any suggestion he made was acknowledged with a grunt, and that was as far as it went.

News of the expedition had by this time become public. The

press had broken the news, in banner headlines, that we planned to build at Huanchaco the largest balsa of totora ever attempted. It was the biggest thing to hit the fishing community within memory, and Don José was the celebrity of the day— as he would be for weeks to come. I had told the press some days before that I hoped to demonstrate that communication between Peru and Mexico had been maintained by sea routes centuries ago, and that the legendary culture heroes Kukulcan of the Maya, Viracocha of the Incas, and Quetzalcoatl of the Aztecs had been a single traveling hero. I had made a composite derived from the three well-known gods and had coined the name "Ku-Vi-Qu" to stress this continuity. To partially finance the voyage I had agreed to write a series of news dispatches to the Lima newspaper *El Comercio* and to give the Columbia Broadcasting System the filming rights to the expedition. They made a one-hour TV film documentary. Assistance from commercial firms had been kept to a minimum because I did not want to lose control as director of the expedition. As a mountain climber I had learned the value of following one leader, when your life may depend on the right decision, which only one person can make. I made it clear that the sponsors were not to dictate decisions.

I had decided on a slow-moving drift-type vessel with a small sail and an A-frame mast rigged on two floats of totora reeds (which experts said would become waterlogged in a matter of thirty days or less) bound by fragile bamboo poles. First, we would build the floats.

At Pisco and Jahuay, south of Lima, totora floats are still being built. It was here that the Curacas of Chincha, according to Pedro Pizarro's account, maintained a fleet of one hundred thousand balsas of totora in the harbor. The reeds are beaten around a central piece of bamboo into "logs," which assures longer life. I had been struck by the use of bamboo centerpieces and asked one of the fishermen why bamboo was used. "Even a snake needs a backbone," he answered. "The bamboo keeps the balsa rigid once it has begun to absorb water." Use of this *corazón* (keel), as it is called, in building an oceangoing balsa seemed the right thing to do. It eliminated one of the major problems which had given me some concern: totora loses its rigidity after becoming waterlogged. This tendency would become dangerous in a larger float weighing hundreds of pounds. The last thing I wanted was to have the totora floats break up under our feet. Use of this centerpiece would help prevent this. Segundo and two men were sent off to the environs of Trujillo to scour the many yards that dealt in woods and bamboos. José instructed them to look for the longest pieces they could find, preferably twenty feet or more, and at least five inches thick. The only cane that could meet these requirements was the *caña de Guayaquil*, the largest and finest grade available. It took several days of hard search to fill the order, but when it was over we had the required canes for the *corazones*.

As the days rolled by, our little boatyard began to fill up with an odd assortment of material. Coils of acaba manila line in varying sizes, from ¼ inch to ¾ inch, were unloaded. We used more than a nautical mile of it—roughly 1,500 pounds; no nails were used; everything was tied by hand. Hemp approximated the old native cordage in preference to the lighter and more economical nylon cord, whose use I forbade for authenticity's sake. Sails of cotton, cut and sewn in Lima, were placed neatly under cover. Stacks of golden totora, a ton or more, glinted in the hot sun. There were 36 *cañas de Guayaquil* for the center of the floats, and 123 selected cane poles of local origin for the under fenders, deck, and superstructure. Each hour brought something new. Yet there never seemed to be enough.

When the author cut these ruins of a circular stone building from the high jungles of northeastern Peru, his attention was drawn to the stepped-Grecque patterns incorporated into the architecture.

The façades of Mitla, 25 miles south of the Monte Alban ruins of Mexico, showed common characteristics with the Peruvian architecture.

Mythological decorations and human heads tenoned in stone walls. Heads are crowned with solar rays or wings, indicating that the figure was of divine origin. Gran Pajatén ruins, Peru.

Quetzalcoatl or Kukulcan was often depicted as a feathered serpent or rattlesnake, as seen here on façade of Uxmal ruins, Yucatán, Mexico.

Stone block found in the Peruvian Andes showing a double-headed coatl serpent design. The sculpture incorporated the rattle, bars and circles, protruding tongue, tears, and doglike face—all Quetzalcoatl symbols.

Profile (left) of woman from Chachapoyas, Peru, is strikingly similar to the classic Maya profile depicted on a stone sculpture (right) from the same area.

(Below left) Detail of stone carving unearthed from jungle ruins in northeastern Peru, believed to represent a civilizing agent known as Viracocha. (Right) Profile of stone carving which indicates that the legendary culture hero of Peru may have been the forerunner of the fair-skinned Chachapoyas civilization.

(Left) *Detail of stone head from Peruvian jungle ruins. Angular spiral at crown and foliated nose were often attributed to Quetzalcoatl.*

(Right) *Coca-chewing Indian porter on one of the author's jungle explorations. A large quid of narcotic plant fills his cheek. He smokes a hand-rolled cigarette.*

(Below left) *Legend says the Chacha people, who built great cities of circular buildings in eastern Peru, were white-skinned. Chacha-poyas girls were famed for their beauty. This one carries on the tradition.* (Right) *Still living in the vicinity of the old ruins, the descendants of the Chacha people are blond and blue-eyed.*

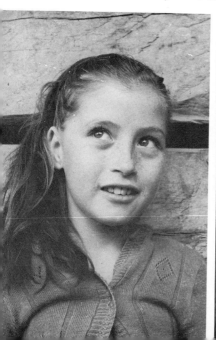

(Left) *This petroglyph found in northern Peru near the great seaports used by the seafaring Lambayeque, Mochica and Chimú is identical to the Mexican hieroglyph for gold.*

(Below) *Cross of the Feathered Serpent found on cliff tomb, northeastern Peru, similar to Quetzalcoatl's cross.*

Detail of mud wall at ruins of Chan Chan.

Aerial photograph of ruined city of Chan Chan, capital of the Chimú civilization. The Chimú were a seafaring people who built boats of reeds.

Caballitos de totora, *little sea horses, one-man floats still used by the fishermen of Huanchaco, Peru. (Photo by Malcolm Burke.)*

Four reed bundles that will form a single float. Taken at the Huanchaco shipyard.

José had put the men to forming the first float. Long stalks of totora were gathered into *puñadas*. Inferior ones were put aside to be given away later. Each of the two floats would be formed of four individual bundles. These would be lashed together to form a single hull. Six *cañas de Guayaquil*, measuring 16½ feet long and 5 inches thick, were selected and tied in two separate lengths (three canes in each). Then the six were tied together by rope end to end to form the *corazón* of the first bundle, called the *madre*, or mother. The totora reeds were placed around it and carefully bound. When this was done, heavy cord was wrapped around the bundle. It required two days to complete the first cigar-shaped bundle. When it was finished, the men stepped back proudly to survey their work. It measured 43 feet in length and was 3 feet thick at the middle. They had sweated in the hot sun. The reed stalks were not casually bound together but forced into place by hammering and pulling. After this was finished they passed a rope around the whole and stuck a long bamboo pole under the rope. Four men put their shoulders against the pole and threw their entire weight against it. Grunting under the effort, they rocked back and forth, the dry totora sending out a crackling and snapping sound. Under maximum contraction, the rope was then knotted securely. Having completed this portion of the job, they went about forming the upward curve of both pointed ends. This was achieved in gradual stages. A bamboo pole was placed under the bundle from either side. Two men then began putting pressure from underneath, forcing the end upward. The process began very near the middle and inched slowly toward the ends. Three men stood on top of the hull near the middle, jumping up and down, their weight forcing the totora to give in to the downward pressure. Two other men stood farther along, toward the point, curving the ends. In this manner the ends were slowly raised. Every so often a worker

would throw water over the totora to make the form permanent. When completed, the float looked like a large slipper, some 36 feet in length, 7 feet shorter because of the new shape.

The work looked promising. There was absolutely no comparison between this fine-looking specimen of totora and the black hulls that had come down from Titicaca. The Indian craftsmen were skilled at knotting cordage and totora. Their hand tools included the bow drill, adze, and saw. Mostly they worked with knife or machete. The *Feathered Serpent* would have no keel, planking, or wooden frames. Reed, line, and bamboo were the materials used—nothing more. The speed and skill of the workers amazed me. Another balsa float was completed by sunset the following day. They made it look incredibly easy. Over the next three days they formed the smaller *hijos* that would lie atop the two larger *madres*. These were slightly shorter, being only 36 feet unbent, and only three *cañas* were placed in the *corazón*.

Some days later the parts for the second hull were finished. Eight magnificent bundles lay on the floor of the yard. There was a strange beauty in the saffron-colored reeds bound with yellow rope. Massive, yet light, each float weighed about 250 pounds at that stage of construction—very little, considering its dimensions.

The first day after completion of the hulls, José and I remained after the men had been sent home for the day. I think the traditions of the coastal Mochica and Chimú are nowhere so evident as in their watercraft. I could see José's face fill with pride as he surveyed what had been accomplished in little over a week's time. Lying there in the fading light, the great bulks of totora looked like giant golden serpents. There was a mystical quality about them, almost as if they had a life of their own. I could understand his sentiments and his attachment to them: the totoras were extensions of himself. Wherever they went, a part of himself would go. Perhaps he saw the construction of the balsa as a means of going beyond the boundaries of his home and village. Whatever it was, he felt there was no one better qualified to build the *Feathered Serpent* . . . and I was secure in the knowledge that if the float failed in its voyage it would not be for José's lack of skill.

The next seven days were filled with hurried activity. The men manhandled the two *madre* floats atop stocks made of large bamboo poles and elevated about a foot off the ground. The *madres* were placed on the left side and lashed close together with ¾-inch manila line. After this the two *hijos* were put on top and lashed to the lower and larger *madres* a little off to one side. When they had finished, the first hull was formed. It measured about 6½ feet wide at the top and was a good bit over 36 feet long. With the addition of the line, I estimated its weight to be about twelve hundred pounds. Then they built the second hull on the right. We had a ton of totora bound with a quarter-ton of line into a pair of strong ocean-going floats.

Next, bamboo was laid out, measured, and cut for the frames and deck. Wraparound belly fenders for the hulls were also prefabricated. The bamboo was not lashed to the hulls, however. We had decided to move the whole lot—hulls and bamboo—to the port of Salaverry, eighteen miles south of Huanchaco, where we would have access to the modern port facilities kindly offered by the Peruvian naval authorities. José and I had concluded that any attempt to put the completed balsa into the water through the breakers at Huanchaco would be a dangerous if not fatal undertaking. The surf might throw the balsa right back onto the beach.

So a big eighteen-wheel flatbed truck was brought in and twenty-five men hired for the job of loading the floats—we did not have the services of a crane at the primitive native Indian community port of Huanchaco. Like Volga boatmen working in unison, the men sweated and strained to the rhythm of grunts and groans and, after much difficulty, got them on the flatbed.

Once we had reached Salaverry, we drove straight to the gates of the modern yards which had been operating for only six years. The guard who came out to examine our papers looked at us with disbelief. Once inside the yards, I heard someone shout, "What in the hell is that!" I could well imagine their surprise at seeing a model of a 2,000-year-old Mochica vessel with an entourage of twenty happy men in the surroundings of a modern port with giant cranes, steel ships, and mechanized loading equipment. To top it off, Segundo, Abilio, and Mercedo were perched atop the great totora hull, waving their arms and shouting, "Make way! The Viracochas are going to sea again!" That was enough to excite the Peruvian stevedores—and not a few of the foreign seamen, who hung over the rails of their ships to see what all the commotion was about.

The port authority had given us ample space in a quiet corner of the yards next to a railway track. It was a perfect place to assemble. But we didn't realize how perfect until a big mechanized crane started to roll down the tracks toward us. Everyone got out of its way. The driver stuck his head out of the cab and yelled down to us, "Where do you want me to put it?"—pointing to the totora hull. It seemed as though nothing had been overlooked by the port officials. Before long, José and the men had stocks built for the hulls. Someone found a five-inch rope and slung it under the hulls. The big crane rolled forward with a grind. The driver lowered the hoist until it was directly above the hull. Three of the men took hold of the tackle and attached it to the rope sling. Slowly the rope and cable were elevated. The line became taut. The hull shuddered, then swung free of the truck. I held my breath for fear a rope would break or the totora would be crushed under the weight. As the crane held the hull a steady five feet above the ground, a dozen pairs of hands swung it around to the right and walked it more than five paces from the truck. Then it was eased down on the stocks and braced with bilgeways. Everyone gave a cheer. My heart skipped a beat with relief.

After this, the flatbed truck was unloaded and was driven away, to return the next day with the second hull. We laid the bamboo poles out alongside the hull and locked tools and other gear away in a shed provided for this purpose. An anchor watch was set, and the men were given the day off. We would begin again the next morning. Segundo, José, and I drove into town to purchase timbers for the mast, rudder, and tiller.

A Witch Blesses the Expedition

Segundo said he was hungry and suggested we eat. There is nothing quite like Peruvian seafood when prepared properly, so I agreed to stop at the first good restaurant, which happened to be a small seaport cafe. I hadn't eaten much of late and was famished. We entered and quickly ordered sea bass covered with tomatoes, onions, and greens. We would begin with raw *seviche* made from corvina and prepared in lemon juice, salt, and hot pepper. Halfway through the meal I had to leave the table and throw up what little I had eaten. Nevertheless, I returned to the table and tried to eat some more. I threw up again but managed to keep some of the food down. My weight had dropped alarmingly fast from my normal 160 pounds to 130. Though very thin, I felt reasonably strong. It was only when I tried to put down some food that I would suffer a tightening of the esophagus—as if there were a fist inside my chest squeezing the life out of me. Worse were the burning sensations that struck every so often. They would come in the middle of the night, my chest and throat seemingly on fire. A medical report showed I had no ulcers and my heart and gall bladder were normal. The doctor who made an examination in the early days, before my condition became chronic, was baffled by my complaints. So I simply endured the pains, hoping they would vanish eventually. They would leave me pale, perspiring, and weak for an hour afterward. I was furious at not knowing the cause.

Once before, an old Peruvian healer or *curandera* living in the jungles had healed me of snakebite with the aid of herbs. So, on the advice of friends in Lima, I agreed to visit one of the more famous *curanderas*—a middle-aged woman, intelligent

and dignified, with very good credentials. On the first visit I
was given dried flower blossoms and leaves from unknown
plants to take as a tea. None of these helped. The second time I
was told to bathe in a red dye—this would surely dispel the
enchantment, for I was presumed to be suffering from *brujería*
(witchcraft: a spell). On my third visit I explained that I was
not responding to treatment. I could not swallow food or liquid.
This statement produced a rather spectacular demonstration.
Had I not known the woman from the two previous visits, I
might have thought her mad. She closed the door to the tiny
consultation room and began circling me while moving her arms
about like a bird flapping its wings. She pursed her lips, making
whistling sounds. Every so often she would jab her long, delicate
fingers in the air as if to accuse some invisible phantom. Then
she stopped as suddenly as she had begun and told me to hold
still. She then stuck several straight pins under the lapels of my
coat to form a cross. Now her mood changed to one of great
calm. She spoke softly, as if to herself: "The enchantment is
strong." Her eyes looked into mine. For the first time I noticed
that her eyes were green. "My herbs cannot alleviate your
problem. You must somehow break the enchantment. But I
shall attempt to help you."

She came from a respected Peruvian family. Her dress, character, and manner showed this. It was said she was well-to-do.
Several rather large diamond rings adorned the fingers of both
hands. I was told she had been responsible for achieving some
remarkable cures among prominent citizens of the community.
The magic arts, both white and black, have been practiced in
Peru for centuries—millennia, if you want to go back to the
Incas and beyond—and they maintain a large following even
today. For these reasons, and my own experiences, I chose to
believe her.

"You are under the influence of a very strong *brujería*," she told me. "Can you remember ever eating any unusual herbs in your food or drink?" I was not prepared for this question. It had been my custom to eat with the natives on expedition. It would have been relatively easy for someone to slip something into my food. But I had many good friends in the interior and could not bring myself to mistrust them.

"It need not be your own native helpers, or even the villagers. It could have been a stranger. I do not know who did it. Only that it was done. Can you not remember having attended a large banquet where many people were gathered?" She was right about the banquets. Goodness knows I had tried to avoid them, but not wishing to offend the villagers I had accepted the more important invitations. "I can't bring myself to believe that anyone would want to poison my food," I said.

"I was not speaking of poison," she replied. "I was speaking of *brujería*. A *brujo* need only put into your food a few specks of matter ground into a fine powder to affect you without your knowing it."

"I don't believe anyone could influence me in this way," I answered.

"Do not disbelieve; you could be bedeviled. Several minds are stronger than a single mind. If a sorcerer managed to put something into your food, something over which incantations had been made, his strength would be manifold. To ally oneself with the deity or the spirits is an old trick of the craft."

"Why would anyone want to do such a thing?"

"Because of your discoveries. The great cities you have wrested from the jungles are monuments to a former great age. It is said that when these old cities come to light again, the Inca empire will rise. The treasures of gold and jewels hidden from the Spaniards will be used to put the Inca back on the throne. You have offended not only the spirits, but the custodians of these secrets as well. Do not believe the *amautas* are dead, Mr. Savoy."

"But I have never desecrated the tombs," I protested.

"It is not important. You have opened the gates."

She focused her eyes on mine again with an intensity that made them shine like emeralds. I had the sensation that they could see right through me. "In one of your major cities, I need not name it, many gather to pray for your failure. It is said that a replica of your person hangs in a secret place. It is dressed in your own clothing, shoes, and stockings, and a photograph of yourself is affixed to the head. Around this image a circle of candles is kept burning day and night. I have been told this. It is safe to say that they are a group of *brujos*. I cannot speak further—only that they meet Tuesdays and Fridays of each week." Her words shocked me. Articles of clothing had been stolen from my home. A copy of a photograph would have been easy to obtain.

I could not bring myself to believe her. And yet, I had been experiencing headaches on the very days she said the meetings took place. It was almost as if someone had put a large bowl over my head. Sounds became muffled; I had dizzy spells when everything would swim before my eyes. Such periods were brief, lasting only a second or two. But the headaches stayed with me for several hours at a time. I had blamed all these symptoms on my weight loss. Now I wasn't sure.

"If the spell is to be broken, we must act quickly." With these words she asked me to sit down on a straight-backed wooden chair. She took a match from a small wooden box and lit a piece of incense and put it into a bowl. The room was soon filled with a sweet aroma. I remembered having once smelled something similar, a scent given off by the *azucena*, a beautiful white lily that grows in the highlands and is gathered by the

Quechua-speaking Indians and sold in the market places. She put a tea kettle on to boil, then sat down across from me with her hands placed flat on a small table. She reached into a drawer of the table and withdrew a small leather pouch, undid the strings, and shook out six green leaves on the table. I instantly recognized them as coca leaves, long used by the Inca priests in divination and chewed by modern Indians for the narcotic effect. She picked them up, three in each hand, and blew over her cupped hands, mumbling something I could not understand. Then she cast all six of them onto the table, much as one would the I Ching wands of the Chinese Confucianists. She was able to read a meaning from the position they assumed on the table. I had seen this form of divination before. Once she was satisfied, she left them where they were and reached over to a small wooden cupboard and took out a cup and dropped four coca leaves on the bottom. Filling it with hot water, she placed it on a saucer and put it down in front of me.

"Drink this coca water," she said. I found myself sipping the mild-flavored concoction, and I was surprised to find I could swallow much more easily than before. I was no stranger to this popular drink used in Peru for all manner of cures, from headache to upset stomach. Taken in small amounts, the plant has no narcotic effect whatsoever.

"The coca leaves tell me that during your expedition by sea you will be challenged. You will be called upon to make a personal sacrifice. But in the end you will overcome. It is good that you are making this trip. By putting water between you and your tormentors, the spell may be broken. There is power in water."

"Then the expedition will be a success?"

"Yes, but not in the way you imagine."

"And what of my illness?"

"Your recovery will depend on whether you break the spell or not."

"You said your herbs would not cure me. What must I do?"

"We have a dilemma. You claim an inability to swallow. Yet, if you do not cleanse your blood of impurities, soon you will die. Here," she said placing a few coca leaves in my hand. "This sacred leaf has been used since time immemorial by the Priests of the Sun. It was not always abused as it is today. Take it whenever you can. It will clothe your body and nourish your spirit. Chew it. You will absorb its vitalizing strength without having to swallow. It will purify your blood and relax your throat muscles. In olden times coca was taken for many reasons. Old seafarers made use of it—it enabled them to drink sea water." She took my hands in her own and pressed them tightly. "Take no heed of your enemies. Now go, Viracocha. I bestow my blessings on your expedition." I offered her payment, but she refused it. I left wondering why she had used that name.

Over the years I had been an explorer of archaeology, anthropology, history, and mythology. I now found myself being transformed into an explorer of metaphysics and philosophy . . . and of myself.

Final Days of Construction

Next day, after we had unloaded the second hull, construction resumed at a furious pace. I begged José to get the *Feathered Serpent* finished before the middle of April, so I could take advantage of the trade winds. He had responded by putting three extra men to work. They began by laying out 17 5-inch-thick guadua canes, *cañas de Guayaquil*. Then they were laid across the hulls. This done, they became *hembras* or females, as they are called. These formed the beams. Four smaller bamboo poles were put in between as ledges. When this was completed, 9 *machos* or male bamboo canes were laid lengthwise. Two lesser ones were put in as mounts for the daggerboards to come later. Atop this went 60 lesser-sized cane *hembras* to form the deck, 47 of which were split to lighten the load. The rounded surfaces were facing upward. The whole was then lashed together by thick cordage joining the hulls. To prevent the line from cutting through the totora, we wrapped 46 smaller bamboo canes under the hulls to serve as fenders. The crane was brought in again to lift the floats so we could do this. Once the job was completed, the frame was lashed securely to the floats around and over the *cañas*. The bamboo fenders would protect the hulls if we struck rocks or had to run up on the beach.

We now had a raftlike platform mounted on a pair of totora floats. Being double-ended, the stern the same as the bow, she was nevertheless beginning to look more like a sea vessel every day. As the days sped by we added four guadua bamboo poles as a support for the A-frame mast or twin sheers I planned to use. A sternpost consisting of four bamboo *cañas* was put in as a support for the *guare* or rudder-oar steering apparatus. Four serpentlike carved wooden figureheads were installed at the bow and stern, lashed to the totora prows or bowsprits. We had strengthened them by adding knightheads made of totora bundles. A Turk's-head was tied to each of the serpent heads. Abilio and Segundo came over and looked at the ornamental knots fagged at the ends, which gave the heads a bearded appearance. Abilio reached up and gave one a tug with his hand. "This one looks like Segundo," he guffawed, taking hold of his companion's black beard with his free hand. Segundo gave him a friendly kick in the seat of the pants and chased him around the balsa.

To keep the curved prows from sagging and to strengthen and stiffen the framework, we stretched spine cables of thick rope along the longitudinal axis of each float over the supporting cane deck and secured them, thus forming two keelsons. The style we used—sandwiching the totora floats in between bamboo poles—made the *Feathered Serpent* half raft and half boat. It was the nearest thing to an old Mochica vessel we could come up with. This increased her overall weight, but since she was an ocean-going craft we wanted durability. The difficult coastline was dangerous, and if we were blown on shore—heaven forbid—I wanted some chance of getting her afloat again. Her speed was bound to be reduced because of the excessive drag. She hadn't been designed for speed in the first place.

José and I agreed to drop a pair of centerboards between the hulls. I had seen well-preserved old daggerboards that had been used in primitive craft dug up from the desert sands. They were called *guares*, and the ones I examined were between two and three yards long and half a yard wide. These were made of huarango or algarroba wood, indigenous trees of the carob family. I had them cut from *caoba* (mahogany) because this was a strong and durable wood. It also happened to be the wood preferred by the native artist who cut and painted them to look like serpent heads. Two and a half yards long, half a yard wide, and one inch thick, they would stand up to the punishment to come later.

Peruvian raft sailors invented an ingenious method of managing their floats by the use of these *guares*. Placed vertically at the bow and stern and pushed down through balsa logs, canes, or totora bundles, they were raised and lowered in such a way as to actually steer the vessel. This was an invention original with the Peruvians and unknown in the rest of the world. Almasa Delano, an American sea captain who happened to observe the use of these *guares* at the Lobos Islands in 1806, wrote:

". . . a catamaran. . . . is formed by a number of large logs together. . . . They are steered by means of large slabs that are put through between the logs, that hold the water like leeboards. In this kind of craft, they beat to windward for many degrees up, sail down the coast, and stretch off from the land thirty or forty miles."

So we dropped two *guares* down between the floats as leeboards. Because the floats were symmetrical, these center-boards would aid the sailing characteristics of the balsa. It was only after much thought and consultation with José that I ordered such additions as the daggerboards. He wouldn't have consented to anything foreign to Mochica boat architects. What amazed me was how easily the shipwrights got the centerboards down through the totora. They hammered and rocked them back and forth with their hands and bare feet, inch by inch, until they were in place. Once the totora became water-soaked there would be no taking them out again. Since they were immovable, we tried to put them in the proper place, about ten percent aft of the gravity sail center, which is rather standard for catamarans; we had no idea of where they had previously been placed, but this location approximated the measurements I had taken from an old ceramic drawing of what I believed to be keels or centerboards on Peruvian double totora balsas. Because of their use and the sail it would not be ac-curate to describe the *Feathered Serpent* as a drift-type vessel in the strictest sense of the term.

Next we put up an A-frame mast consisting of two spars joined at the top. These were anchored on the transverse bam-boo base. They measured $16\frac{1}{2}$ feet in length, and when standing gave the mainmast a height of $14\frac{1}{2}$ feet. I should have used mangle (mangrove) or chonta, the hard trunk of a palm in-digenous to the jungles, transported over the Andes in olden times and used as masts and daggerboards. I selected Oregon pine in honor of my home state, since chonta was not available and it would not lessen the authenticity of the balsa (the masts were not hollow but solid, which added 165 pounds to the overall weight). A bamboo cane 29 feet long was selected for the head. This was designed to carry our large lateen or lug sail obliquely on the mast spars if ever needed. The cotton sail measured 28½ feet in length by 13½ feet at the foot and represented a lot of canvas. We also had a smaller lateen sail measuring about 20 square meters, and a square sail with the same quantity of canvas. We cut a smaller head and yard for these sails. The square sail served us best and was used more than any other. (We also had Dacron and nylon sails for emergencies, in the event the cotton ones were ripped by wind or washed overboard.)

Pedro Asabache, now a famous Peruvian Indian painter, who was master of a school of art, volunteered to paint polychrome Mochica designs on the sails. He was an old friend who had given me the use of his home in Moche, not far from the pyramids, during my early years in Peru. We often spent the nights talking about such a sea voyage as this one. When the bright-colored sails were brought in by truck and unfurled, they excited the Huanchaqueros no end. They all wanted photographs of themselves against these sails. There were stripes of red, yellow, green, and black topped by a Mochica runner at the peak. Black-and-white checkerboard design made up the base, with brown pelicans in the white squares. It was truly beautiful. The second lateen was smaller but painted in the same way. Our square sail had been painted in transverse stripes of yellow at the top followed by green, red, blue, then yellow, and finally black. Later, at Talara, we added a large sunburst in orange paint, right in the center, that had somehow been forgotten by Pedro.

Old Azcona, José's brother, the authority on marlinspike

seamanship, put up six shrouds, three forestays, and three back-stays from the deck to the mast in order to support the latter. He had wisely put in a strong towline lashed to the frame and guylines for later hoisting should it be necessary. He knotted a Jacob's ladder for the portside. One afternoon he went up the ladder and tied a crosstree to the masthead to support two flagged ropes to serve as weathervanes. He extended the mast by throwing up three pieces of bamboo with a truck at the head for the flags and pennants we would carry. He also tied a hand-carved wooden block to the mast for the halyard. Since no metals, bolts, or nails were used in the construction, the craft became a museum of cordage and knots. He instructed Segundo and me in the care of line. Being of vegetable fiber, our manila line would require special care. We learned how to keep it dry and clean for proper stowing; to watch out for chafe and abrasion; to keep out kinks and to coil it in such a way that sun and air got to it. While Segundo and I were both familiar with rope, we listened attentively, knowing that our lives might well depend on our knowledge of it. He taught us how to make a line to a pile; the correct way of making fast to a cleat; how to secure a line to a hook or towline. We had a sew-ing kit on board with spike, twine, needle, palm, and sail canvas. Azcona taught us the basics of repairing sail, and when he had finished, we felt much more like seamen.

We thought it best to use a sweep oar for steering. This kind of steering apparatus was used on old balsa rafts as well as the daggerboard method mentioned earlier. As for the mast, I had already selected Oregon pine, though José wanted me to use huarango or algarroba wood—a good idea, but I didn't want to have any further delays; we were behind schedule as it was. It made such little difference that I told the woodworker to go ahead and cut out a steering oar sixteen-odd feet long, with a blade three feet wide, along with a spare for emergencies. When they arrived days later, I found the blade barely twelve inches wide, which was far too narrow, and I told him so. He explained that the navigator had told him that what I wanted was too wide. I had gone to great lengths to plan every detail of the balsa's construction carefully. Any deviation might very well cause us incalculable harm. Once before when I had asked the navigator to work with the sailmaker, somehow the sails that came back did not follow my sketches. It was too late to do much about it, so we had to cut the yards accordingly, much smaller than planned. Now we had a steering oar and a spare with very small blades. We could only hope they would work. The men tied the oar in place and fit it snugly into the thole pins. The spare was readied and lashed onto the balsa's starboard side. Two extra centerboards and two figureheads had been put in on the portside. Every effort was made to keep her carefully balanced. The yards and the extra bamboo cane for repairs were weighed by hand before being lashed in place on either side.

On Easter Sunday, April 6th, the port authority ordered the *Feathered Serpent* lowered by crane into the water. This was to test her buoyancy and determine her draft. So, at ten-fifteen in the morning, the big crane lumbered down the rails toward us. Lines were attached, and the balsa was lifted and carried airborne to the dock. She was put into the water fifteen minutes later with four hands on board. She floated with a flair, much to the surprise of the large crowd gathered on the dock. When José took a measurement and found her displacement to be just under six inches, even when six other men came on board, we tried to rock her to and fro, but she remained steady as a rock— a common feature of catamaran design.

The events of the previous ten days had been filmed by a CBS News film crew headed by correspondents Charles Kuralt and David Burke, both of whom had participated in one of my

El Dorado expeditions the year before. Now they were following up on the story of possible links between Peru and Mexico.
They were accompanied by Tom Spain, cameraman, and Don
Aldrich, soundman. Kuralt came on board and expressed delight in her buoyancy. "She floats high and dry," he said to me.
No stranger to the sea, an amateur yachtsman in his own right,
he liked the feel of the *Feathered Serpent*. "I'll bet she surfs
over the big ones," he said admiringly. "How I wish I were
going with you."

A few minutes later the *Feathered Serpent* was raised, then
lowered into the water again at the request of CBS. I saw no
harm in this but cautioned the crane operator to maintain tension on the cable to prevent the fragile balsa from crashing into
the piers because of a strong wind and current. Later I took
time for an interview with Kuralt when the balsa was returned
to her berth.

Time was running short. The men from Huanchaco, led by
José, had obtained permission from the port authority to work
at night. Floodlights were erected and we worked nearly
around the clock to get the balsa completed before the fifteenth.

Segundo's contribution to the balsa's construction up to this
point had been negligible. He was not a boat builder; he knew
nothing of totora. He had never been to sea, but with the same
enthusiasm he had shown in the jungles, he fell to work wherever he was needed. When it was time to put up the deckhouse
he was given a free hand as ship's carpenter. I had asked for a
circular shed at least 8 feet in diameter, but with the ingenuity
typical of a man accustomed to making things fit, he made it
oblong, 13 feet long and 8 feet wide. I was quite pleased, because our deck had a beam of only 13½ feet and an overall
length of about 18 feet. The hut fit snugly under the A-frame,
leaving enough space for us to negotiate the sides when going
fore and aft. For the roof he used red willow branches tied with

cord and thatched with totora. It was to hold up throughout the voyage against heavy seas and torrential rains, keeping the expedition's gear and provisions as well as all hands as dry as a bone. Two bamboo bunks were built with stowage space below and space for a third man on the floor next to the bunks— sufficient space, since one man would always be on watch, leaving the other three free.

Abilio and Mercedo were fairly receptive to the idea of going along. I needed a four-man crew to manage the balsa safely and would have taken a fifth if possible. This would have cut down the time a man would have to stand watch. More important, Abilio and Mercedo were experienced watermen and carpenters. Without their skills our chances of reaching our destination were minimal.

José's Fall

Any thoughts I might have had of taking on these two men disappeared on the evening of Saturday, April 12, when José, who was putting the finishing touches on the shrouds at the masthead, fell to the deck fifteen feet below. The Huanchaqueros rushed him to the hospital, where eight stitches were taken in his forehead. His tremendous arms had broken the fall but were fractured below the elbows. The doctor gave strict orders that he be confined to his hospital bed until after we sailed.

Later I drove out to Huanchaco. The Huanchaqueros were clustered at the front door of José's house when I arrived. Abilio was there with Mercedo and nine or ten men. I told them how sorry I was about the accident, but that we must go ahead with the completion of the balsa. They didn't seem overly interested, and when I asked Abilio if he wanted to go with us, one of the older men, who seemed to assume leadership in the absence of José, turned a pair of dark eyes on me and said: "It is bad enough to have the blood of Don José on your balsa. Would you ask him for his son, too?" I turned and looked at Abilio.

"I am sorry, Señor Savoy, but my mother will not let me go."

I was thunderstruck. Mercedo buried his chin in his chest. The rest just looked at me with empty faces.

This had happened to me before on expedition. A mule loses its footing and plunges over an embankment. The rivers overflow their banks before the appropriate time. A porter spots a human skull placed by superstitious natives on a rock near the main trail. One of the men comes down with sickness. Any kind of freak accident, such as José's fall, will spook an expedition. I knew it was useless to ask any of the Huanchaqueros to join us. It was all over and I knew it. I thanked them and got back into my car and drove to Trujillo. I was incapable of speaking to anyone and didn't stop even to see José. I went straight home and fell into a dreamless sleep, exhausted from the events of the day.

Just after sunrise next day I went out to Salaverry as usual. The sun was coming up over the Pyramid of the Moon, giving the sand a radiant glow. The wind from the sea sent big swells against the beach. I drove past the docks in the morning calm. The large crane hoists were quiet. Nothing seemed to move. One could hear the slap of the water against the piers and the distant cries of sea gulls. From a distance the *Feathered Serpent* looked like a ghost ship. It was strange not to see men tending her. The place was deserted, and there was a strange, almost ominous, stillness about the yards. Fittingly, it was Sunday the thirteenth. When I pulled up I was surprised to see Segundo standing on the portside of the balsa. Parking the car, I climbed up on deck. He stood looking down at a red splotch on the bamboo.

"That's where he hit. Imagine," he said, "all the way from the masthead. It's a miracle he wasn't killed."

"Have you seen José?" I asked.

Segundo seemed lost in thought. Then he began to laugh. "He's a mummy. An absolute mummy."

"A mummy, you say?"

"*Dios mío*, Gene, you should see what those doctors have done to poor José. Why, he couldn't get out of bed if he wanted to. He's wrapped up in fifty kilos of bandages." Then he began to laugh again, almost hysterically. "A blood sacrifice, that's what it is."

No disrespect toward José was intended. It isn't unusual to see jungle folk laughing at such things. They never show misery and will laugh even when they themselves are injured. I've seen them smile at the funerals of their own children. This doesn't mean they aren't capable of suffering. Outsiders find it difficult to understand. I watched Segundo's antics—wrapping up his arms and face in an old newspaper—in imitation of José's condition. Suddenly I found myself laughing with him. Thank goodness no one was around to hear us. While it helped ease the tension for a few minutes, we knew we were in real trouble.

While we were feeling sorry for ourselves, José was taken by the Huanchaqueros from the hospital to his home. He had attempted to get out of bed and visit the balsa but was held down by his wife and friends. He had made them promise to help ready the balsa for sailing. He gave them a lecture, saying that the reputation of the village was at stake. They all swore to do as he wished.

Abilio came to my room that evening to tell me the good news. I couldn't have been happier. There was no mention of anyone's going with us. Later I held a palaver with Segundo and the navigator to make a decision about whether to go ahead or not. Dressed in a red shirt and white slacks, Segundo looked spotless as usual. The navigator always wore the same thing— a pair of old coveralls, a limp, wrinkled shirt, and a new pair of deck shoes drawn from the expedition's stores. Talking in his high-pitched nasal Spanish, the navigator said we didn't need the Huanchaqueros and that we could handle the balsa alone. When I asked Segundo what he thought, he said that if I decided to go ahead he would accompany me. He had given his word to do so. Whatever else could be said for them, they both displayed genuine courage that night. I was used to seeing it in Segundo. In the case of the navigator, it was a pleasant surprise. That settled it. The expedition was on again.

Final Preparations

Abilio and a full team of workers showed up Monday morning. They piled out of the old flatbed truck and went to work as if nothing had happened. José's presence was missed, but I tried not to think about that.

At nine-thirty, Commander José Noriega, captain of the port, paid us an unexpected visit. While the shipwrights went about their daily tasks, we did our best to show him around. Newspaper reporters festooned with tape recorders and cameras crowded around, thrusting microphones at him and flashing pictures. After he was satisfied that we were seaworthy, he said the balsa would have to be put into the water today and spend the night—fully loaded—at the mole. I protested. I saw no reason for the extra risk of having her dashed against the pier by wind and current. But it was to no avail. She would have to go into the water for twenty-four hours before permission to sail would be granted. I looked at the elder Huanchaqueros. That meant they would have to ready the balsa by noon. They made faces and shook their heads but went on with their work.

A spray gun was brought in by the Huanchaqueros with several one-gallon containers. They argued that traditional totora balsas were always coated with several layers of varnish to protect the totora from being eaten away by sea creatures and to avoid just plain rotting. There was no evidence that varnish had been used on balsas in ancient times, but in the end I allowed a single thin coat to be applied to the outer surfaces and to the bamboo platform—for tradition's sake, and to keep the men happy. I knew it would soon be chipped away by the sea. The thought of the totora being eaten by sea creatures was a new worry. I was told such creatures abounded in the waters of Ecuador.

The floats, bamboo platform, and all knotted rope were thoroughly checked out by a team under the direction of Azcona. Segundo and Abilio installed the galley on the starboard side amidships next to the cabin: a wooden cutting table, bamboo locker for stores, and a rack for the LPG fuel stove with insulating board behind. We would have liked to use a charcoal burner for cooking, the ancient method, but decided it was not safe. Our reed and bamboo balsa was highly inflammable as it was. We stored extra bottles of fuel on the port side, along with a second stove and two emergency kerosene Primus hand-pump stoves which had served us so well on field expeditions. Later, I often caught Segundo, who served as cook, throwing what he considered unnecessary items into the sea to lighten the load. Like all jungle people, he believed in traveling light and getting to his destination as quickly as possible. If he had had his way, we would have eaten nothing but raw fish and dry cereal. When I would point to a string of boxes bobbing up and down on the sea behind the balsa, he would shrug his shoulders and go about his routine as if nothing had happened.

By noon the *Feathered Serpent* was ready for the crane, which came lumbering down the rails. At twelve-forty she was dropped quietly onto the water on the sheltered leeside of the dock not far from the seagoing tug that was waiting to give us the tow out to sea on the morrow. We moored the balsa about ten feet from the dock with an after bowline. With a flagging of the wind she went ahead, and the port-bow figure-head was nearly twisted off the bowsprit. The throng of spectators lined up on the pier gave out a groan, but Abilio and Mercedo quickly pushed her out again with a long bamboo pole. While they were doing this, two Huanchaqueros came aboard and expertly threw stern, bow, and forward quarterlines over the upper piles, also tightening the after bowline around the forward bitt, bringing her within five feet of the pier. She was now lying comfortably at her berth. Enough slack was kept in the lines to allow for shifts in tide, wind, and current without letting her move away from the dock. As a precaution, a stern line was put out from the tug to a buoy to keep the tug from swinging around in a circle and smashing into the delicate *Feathered Serpent*.

Afloat, the *Feathered Serpent* was a beautiful thing. In a way it seemed a pity to take her to sea, knowing that her graceful lines would be distorted by the pounding waves, her golden color darkened by wind and spray. It was like taking a flower and throwing it over a waterfall. How majestic she appeared at anchorage against the dingy brown and pale gray of the piers. The red-and-white serpent figureheads—the colors of the *Feathered Serpent*, be it known as Kukulcan of the Maya, Vira-cocha of the Incas, or Quetzalcoatl of the Aztecs as well as modern Peru—matched the white desert sands turned a fiery red by the blazing sun. It was as if the mythological phoenix from ancient Heliopolis, dedicated to the sun god Ra, had its Peruvian equivalent and had returned to the altar of a Mochica temple to burn itself, only to arise from its own ashes in modern times. Here again was the giant bird with golden wings and jeweled plumage, more magnificent than ever, ready to take flight to the sun temples of the north. It had no other purpose. This was the sole reason for its existence.

Now only the stores remained to be put on board. As a condition for granting us port clearance the port authority had demanded that we take water and stores to last the crew at least 110 days, in addition to navigational equipment and radio transmitter with receiver! A dozen Huanchaqueros gathered to help with the stowing of provisions and supplies—more than a ton of boxes, cans, packets, and assorted gear. I checked off the items one by one from the expedition's manifest, a copy of which had been given to the captain of the port. The list seemed endless. By forcing so many provisions upon us, the authorities were unwittingly endangering our chances of success. With all this extra weight the *Feathered Serpent* was now more of a cargo raft than anything else, and we would have to depend on trade winds and the Peruvian current to carry us along.

Needless to say, the effect on the interior of the deckhouse was devastating. First, over a hundred gallons of fresh water in polyethylene containers was jammed under the starboard bunk, stacked along the portside, and the rest pushed under the bunk at the forward part of the cabin. Spare sails, sea anchors, rigging and coils of rope, boat hook, heaving lines, hand lead and lines were stowed on the foredeck next to the deckhouse. Boxes of canned food, some thousand cans in all, were put in against the plastic containers as protection against possible damage. Two large wooden kegs filled with foodstuffs were placed on either side of the deckhouse just outside the opening aft. Rice, sugar, flour, coffee, salt, tea, dried milk and other perishable foodstuffs that had to be kept dry were put into plastic bags and then stowed in the deckhouse wherever there was room. Handsaw, machete, sail-repair kit, and emergency canisters for converting sea water into fresh water were put into lockers near the door. The emergency rubber dinghy lifeboat was lashed to the overhead. We also put up lifelines around the deckhouse, with a life preserver and canvas bucket on each side. Under one of the two bunks each man had a locker in which he placed his own rubber life preserver, waterproof band, towels, toilet items, flashlight, whistle, foul-weather gear, extra clothing, twine, pocket knife, jacket, sleeping bag, waterproof wristwatch, books, paper and pencils, emergency reserve of food, and other personal items. Segundo outfitted his galley by tying several utensils of his own selection—rustproof knives, forks, wooden spoons, gourds and wooden bowls—on the side of the working table near the stove. He wrapped his own special herbs he used for cooking in plastic bags and stowed them in his personal locker, along with a large supply of matches, fishhooks, and line. A five-gallon container of gasoline for the storm lanterns was stowed on deck on the port side near the deckhouse. It was covered with canvas, and a fire extinguisher placed alongside it. We carried two twelve-point lanterns, a red one for the port side and a green one for starboard. A thirty-six-point white hurricane lamp was carried at the stern. Since we would be in the shipping lanes, proper lighting at night could help prevent collision—one of our greatest fears. For additional safety, I installed a light metal passive radar reflector at the masthead which could be picked up by radar-equipped ships frequenting the Pacific coasts of South and Central America. Inside the deckhouse, above the lintel, I tied a hand-crank type of foghorn within easy reach of the helmsman on watch. A lifesaving flare pistol with a variety of shells was put in my locker under the starboard bunk. Perhaps ancient Mochica and Chimú sailors didn't require such things, but they did not have to contend with large ships of steel hundreds of feet long, traveling at fast speeds. In this respect true duplication of an ancient voyage was not possible.

The expedition's navigational instruments, including a sextant, magnetic compass, hand-bearing compass, barometer, chronometer, anemometer, instruments for piloting, patent log, charts, light list, tidal and current tables, and pilot book, plus assorted aids, were stowed below the starboard bunk in a special locker and entrusted to the care of the navigator. I had selected a good battery-operated marine radio receiver for an hour or two of daily music. I had used walkie-talkie two-way communication units on my field expeditions and felt there was a genuine use for them with our small crew. In an emergency the rubber dinghy could be sent ashore to maintain ship-to-shore communication or in case we needed to forage for food or water. Though I understood the value of a marine radio-telephone for communication with other boats and with shore stations, I wanted to keep the world as much removed as possible. So I settled on a short-range Citizens Band Radio with a reliable range of only five to fifteen miles. With little chance of a signal's being picked up, I felt we were insulated. This, I thought, was sufficient to satisfy the needs and demands of the port authority, although it wouldn't have satisfied any boatman under normal circumstances, much less myself. At the urging of CBS I agreed to take a rescue-emergency transmitter in the event we were carried out to sea or caught in the doldrums near the Galápagos Islands. It was stowed away in a watertight container along with an atlas of the South Pacific islands.

The Huanchaqueros came aboard to complete their work. Two ten-foot *caballitos* of totora, with one end truncated and the other curved, were lashed to either side along with a split bamboo paddle. I doubt if they would have been of much use in an emergency, but they were highly decorative and they did serve as fenders. By twelve-thirty the steering oar was in place and the shipwrights went ashore, satisfied that they could do no more. They promised to return next day for the launching. The *Feathered Serpent* was heavy in the water, with her waterline down another twelve inches. Her draft was now nearly eighteen inches—far too much. We reshuffled the stores a little aft to bring her bow up. (I feared she would be swamped as she was towed out to sea.) This would help her sailing characteristics, too, I thought, and would prevent her from sailing down by the head. As it was, I envisioned a slow passage and began to ponder how to lighten her.

After the men left, Segundo and the navigator tidied up the balsa. They picked up shavings of bamboo and bits of rope and threw them into a pail for later collection. Rope was coiled and the balsa put in proper order. In the meantime, I concerned myself with the flags and ensigns to be used. The *Feathered Serpent* represented an expedition sponsored by the Andean Explorers Club. I had decided very early to let the *Feathered Serpent* be known and recognized by her own flag and pennant —the colors of our club and of the legendary folk hero Viracocha-Quetzalcoatl. There would be time enough, on the high seas, to break out the Stars and Stripes of her skipper's homeland. I stowed the flags and pennants in my own locker and turned my attention to the still- and motion-picture cameras, film, and sound equipment to be taken with us.

I had my own 35mm cameras—two Nikons with several lenses and two waterproof Nikonos cameras (the only cameras to survive the voyage), lightmeters and a waterproof box of color and black-and-white Kodak film. These were carefully placed in a foam-rubber box with a good amount of silica gel to keep out dampness. Everything was put into individual plastic bags as an added precaution. CBS had given me a Bolex

16mm motion-picture camera plus an extra Bell & Howell camera, along with thousands of feet of film on hundred-foot rolls. I had used a motion-picture camera before, having put together documentaries of my own in earlier days. They also gave me a tape recorder with cassettes.

After this I put a two-kilo bag (about four pounds) of select coca leaves in my locker for tea, or, if I felt like it, to chew, as the *bruja* had recommended. On expedition I occasionally stuffed a few leaves in my mouth to join the men, who chewed it not only as a stimulant but as a preventive against enchantment during jungle explorations. When taken as tea it is a very mild stimulant, far more satisfying than coffee or tea and probably less harmful. I never added quicklime because it burned my tongue and the inside of my mouth. And I did not fancy the green lips and black teeth of those who chew it regularly. I have seen my porters carry a forty-pound load over rough country, cutting their way with machete through thick vegetation growing at altitudes of 10,000 to 13,000 feet above sea level, for long periods of time without any food. Though they are small of stature, some barely reaching five feet and weighing less than a hundred pounds, the endurance and stamina of these porters was astounding. Coca leaves must have given them some inner strength to go on where others would have dropped from sheer exhaustion. Some of my most trusted and responsible men used coca, though they were not addicted to it.

Afterward I made a routine check of the balsa to see if she was ready to sail. I found everything in order, checking off one by one my list of "things to do." Next, I assigned watches. We had agreed on two four-hour watches per man. With this arrangement one man would take the helm for four hours, leaving the other two free to rest and attend to routine duties. Each of us had his work cut out from the very beginning.

Segundo had the galley. The navigator his navigational duties: He was to take regular bearings and plot our course on the chart; he was to make his report each afternoon before going on watch. I would handle the photography, take notes, keep the official expedition log, and make observations. I would plot our course, based on my dead reckonings when in sight of the coast-line. These would be compared to those of the navigator. In addition we had regular duties: keeping the balsa seaworthy, fishing, maintaining lookout, and other routine tasks. When the assignments were completed, I explained very carefully to both Segundo and the navigator that the safety of the crew would come first at all times, that I would tolerate no risks of life. I stressed that we would have to work as a team. I emphasized that this was an expedition, and not simply a sea voyage by balsa. Barring any unforeseen illness or accident that might alter the situation, I would direct the expedition to a successful conclusion.

While we were talking, a car drove up on the dock, and, much to our surprise, out stepped the captain of the port, asking permission to board. Quick hands on the dock took hold of the painter and inched us up to the dock. Down jumped the captain, piped aboard with due ceremony by Segundo playing something that sounded like Inca notes on a bosun's pipe I had given him. We shook hands, and then he made a tour of the balsa's platform and deckhouse, expressing satisfaction with what he saw. He commented on our spirit of adventure, saying he would not care to undertake such a trip with all the discomforts facing us. Perhaps the thought of going with us made him think in terms of modern navigation, for he turned to me and said: "Officially the ship's company will be as follows: The commander [our navigator] will be captain. The crew will consist of yourself as chief of the expedition and Segundo Grandez as helmsman." Then he wished us luck and started to leave.

I was too flabbergasted to say anything at first. It had to be a joke. "Captain," I said, "I beg your pardon. I am the director of the expedition, am I not?"

"Yes."

"Well, the balsa and the expedition are one. How can the navigator be skipper?"

He turned and said in an offhand way, almost casually, "The navigator is a *capitán de fragata* [commander] like myself and a blue-water sailor. We must have a good navigator in charge if you are to sail."

"But, sir, navigation by instruments is superfluous on a coastal voyage like this one. I have complied by taking a navigator as a precaution, and we have all signed the disclaimer statement for the port authority, so no one is responsible for our lives but ourselves. You have our voyage plan. I cannot turn command over to anyone!"

I continued to protest, but in vain.

"You are carrying the Peruvian flag. There are regulations. I cannot let you sail under any conditions other than those I have stipulated. Technically, the navigator is to be captain, at least in Peruvian waters."

Did he have orders from Lima? I never did find out. When I threw a glance at the navigator, he was grinning. The captain of the port shook my hand, then departed with the words, "The commander will take you where you want to go. The tugboat *Salaverry* has orders to see you out into open water whenever you wish."

Later Segundo sauntered up alongside and put a hand on my shoulder: "We all know who the chief is." The last thing I wanted was a complicated problem, especially over command. If the navigator was qualified, as he said he was, then I had everything to gain from his presence. I decided to be impartial. Now ready for the sea with the supposed blessing of the port,

I issued orders to start off-loading six hundred pounds of surplus stores. The balsa was simply too low in the water and had to come up a good six inches. I was determined to use my own judgment henceforth. If we ran short of food and water, rain and plenty of fish would be available. When this was completed, Segundo and I drove out to Huanchaco to visit José. The navigator was left on anchor watch.

José was feeling much better and the stitches had been removed from his head. His arms were black and swollen above the bandages. We talked about the *Feathered Serpent*, how beautiful and seaworthy she looked, her draft, and the events that had taken place. He apologized about not being able to send his son with us. I understood and did not press him about it. He had taken out an old chart of the coastline, telling me everything he knew and what he had been able to learn from the Huanchaqueros. He warned me to stay west of the Island of Lobos de Tierra and east of Lobos de Afuera, to steer a course that would take the balsa between them. We had discussed the dangerous waters in the area of Talara and north of Cabo Blanco. He particularly urged getting far out to sea when sailing the Gulf of Guayaquil because of the great tidal currents. Beyond that he was not knowledgeable. But he had given me enough information about the part of the coast he knew to serve me well. When we finally said good-bye I thought I saw a pair of misty eyes looking at me. He had proved to be a grand friend and one I would remember with fondness all my life.

I returned to the *Feathered Serpent* to stand watch. The deckhouse was dry and comfortable and the balsa was very steady. Yet I did not sleep well and my dreams were troubled.

Next morning at daybreak we dressed the ship in a rainbow of pennants and ensigns. The pennant of the Andean Explorers Club was hoisted, along with the red-and-white streamers of the *Feathered Serpent* expedition. Segundo hoisted a Peruvian

flag, and I saw the navigator break out a small Italian ensign
and run it up one of the spars. The balsa had been christened
the day before by breaking an imitation Mochica pottery vase,
which by local custom was thrown from the dock onto the
balsa. Unfortunately ours missed and splashed into the water.
Segundo had completed the ceremony by breaking the vase
with a bamboo pole. For decoration several pieces of pottery—
actually coin banks which had been donated by a local bank—
were tied around the deckhouse. Most ornamental, I thought;
they lent charm to the balsa, if nothing else. From a distance
they looked like the real thing. A local artisan from Moche had
shaped, painted, and fired them using the same techniques as his
ancestors, and it was hard to tell which was genuine when
one of his pieces was placed alongside a very old pot. He told
me that he had sold not a few to United States and European
museums, which displayed them as authentic pieces—without
the coin slot, of course. He thought this a big joke. His remarkable ability was later to cause the expedition some em-
barrassment.

A crowd estimated at four thousand lined the quay. They
gave a great cheer when the Peruvian flag went up. Segundo,
being the only national, was the hero of the day. I instructed
him to cast off the lines. A mighty *"Viva el Peru!"* went up in a
single shout as we moved from the dock. He waved and went
forward to heave a line to the waiting tug. Moments later the
Feathered Serpent was in tow by the oceangoing *Salaverry*.
Several smaller boats escorted us out of the harbor through
large swells. The fishing boat *Rigel*, serving as a camera boat for
CBS, lay behind to record the events of that morning of April
15, 1969.

Twenty minutes later, at eleven-thirty and a little more than
a nautical mile offshore, the towlines were dropped. The *Salaverry* gave a farewell blast on her foghorn, all hands from the

—◆►—

Drifting Along the Peruvian Current

First Crisis at Sea

With the wind at her tail, the *Feathered Serpent* lumbered along a good 10 miles offshore. We were following the natural bulge of the South American continent which juts out into the Pacific at this point. To get around the bulge we had to bear 125 miles west before cutting north across the Gulf of Guayaquil and hopefully on to Manta, Ecuador. The weather had been warm closer in. As we pulled away from the desert and the hot winds that blew across it, a chill was in the air. We were now in the grip of the Peruvian current, and the cold waters carried up from Antarctica were pulled to the surface by the rotation of the earth. Because of this the sea settled into a series of undulating swells that jarred the bowsprits as they passed under the balsa. I had staked my reputation, fortune, and possibly my life on the belief that wind and current would carry our fragile vessel to Central America.

With the *Rigel* right behind, following in our wake and observing our progress, we were propelled by the lateen at a good three knots. I had been used to handling a Marconi cat rig, as gentle as a feather to the touch. By comparison, the *Feathered Serpent* was sluggish and slow to answer the helm.

The navigator was having great difficulty in moving the sweep oar. The ship had turned fractious and was bearing north— a course that would put us on the beach in three hours or less if we didn't alter it. We had attached one-inch lines above the oar blade about halfway down from the steering oar on both sides. These lines were then brought up and put through a wooden pulley on both the port and starboard sides and then tied to the oar just above the thole pins so the helmsman could handle them. If one wanted to steer to starboard, the helm had to be put over the port, or, to steer to port, one moved the helm to starboard. Without the lines it would have been impossible for one man to handle the big sixteen-foot steering oar against the pounding sea. Once the lines were pulled and the oar secured in the desired position, the ship would pretty well steer itself, with only an occasional correction by the helmsman.

This was the theory. But in fact the helmsman was not able to swing the steering oar alone or to secure the lines. The navigator threw his weight against the helm (he was a large man, well over two hundred pounds), moving it to starboard. But before he could secure the line, a big swell would come in from the west and ram the balsa, throwing the oar back to the opposite side. She would sail eccentrically and then point her bow to shore again. Try as he might, the navigator could not handle the oar alone. Segundo and I came running over to help. It took all three of us to bring the oar over to starboard and secure it. We could see that this arrangement was going to offer serious problems. We had counted on one man at a time on the helm, leaving the other two free to sleep and to carry out other duties. The balsa lacked maneuverability and was troublesome to sail. Her performance was disappointing. If we couldn't steer we were in serious trouble.

We fought to put the sweep oar back to port. It moved very slowly. When it was in position, I was shocked to see that the

Feathered Serpent persisted in bearing down on the land. She was out of control! Being multi-hulled, she didn't heel over when the wind struck the sail; the wind was transformed to driving power. The ability to sail faster than the true wind speed is a well-known characteristic of catamarans. I didn't expect to see it happen on our heavy craft. This was a dangerous situation, and night was falling.

First spilling the wind, then dowsing the sail, I called for help. Both Segundo and the navigator were seasick, so I furled it alone. It was senseless to try going on under these conditions. I decided then and there to drift along with the current the rest of the night and try to find the difficulty on the morrow. The *Rigel* was standing by and could take us in tow in any emergency, but I would not ask her to unless it was absolutely necessary. We were drifting nicely and were well enough out to sea so that there was no danger of being put on shore.

The sun sank into the western ocean. We filled the lamps with kerosene. While we were doing this a small boat came over from the *Rigel*, standing well off to film the activities. Just before dark it returned to the ship. I was glad to see it go. The fumes from the kerosene gave me nausea. No one wants to look down the lens of a camera when seasick. We could make out the running lights of our escort, which moved about us like a mother hen caring for a stray chick. It was reassuring to know she was there. During my watch I analyzed the situation: The problem had to be the sweep oar. The blade was too narrow. I thought of lashing on the extra keel. But when I looked for it, it wasn't there. Someone had removed it at Salaverry when we were off-loading. It was imperative that we repair the sweep oar—and fast. There was only one thing to do: make port the following day; otherwise we would risk the whole expedition. One advantage to coastal navigation is that you can make landfalls when necessary. On the other hand, in ancient times landfalls were part of the risk of coastal sailing: Every sailor knows the beating a ship takes when making port—particularly so with old-time sailing vessels such as our fragile balsa.

By drifting along on the Peruvian current we could tell whether it ran parallel to shore or swept out to sea. That night I slept on deck to keep an eye on the *Rigel*. At 0100 the stern light went out and I pumped up the lamp and got it started again. The *Rigel* was still there, about a quarter mile off the port stern. Was she drifting along the current too? I did not hear the sound of her engine. Her generator was running, however, and I lay there listening to it and taking catnaps. Segundo and the navigator were seasick, so I chose not to awaken them. I brewed a cup of hot coca tea. After that I felt much better.

The sun came over the Andes far to the east. A clear blue sky and darker blue sea enveloped us. I was stiff and tired, and my joints ached from the damp air. But now that the sun was out I was beginning to feel better. We were drifting along about ten miles off shore, the same as the day before. Taking out my walkie-talkie, I called up the *Rigel*. I was astounded to hear they'd had a difficult time keeping up with the *Feathered Serpent*. The old sailors were much impressed. Captain Baylón's crackling, static-filled voice told me that we were not far from Puerto Chicama, that we had covered sixty nautical miles, mostly by drift. I explained the problems we were having with the lateen sail and the steering oar and requested that they send the dory over with the CBS cameramen. A few minutes later the little boat came bobbing over the waves like a cork, sometimes fading from sight in one of the large troughs, only to reappear again at the crest of a wave.

Tom Spain stood at the stern taking shots with his movie camera. Dan Aldrich was at the oars. They came alongside and threw us a line. Minutes later they stepped aboard. I let them get the feel of the deck and make a routine inspection of the balsa before making my report. "She is more steady than the *Rigel*," said Tom Spain, amazed at her stability. "And drier, too," added Dan, adjusting one of the small hand microphones of his tape recorder. I explained our situation and asked if they could take the *Rigel* to port and drive to Huanchaco for Abilio, a carpenter, and the missing daggerboard. "We'll head for Chicama," I said, "and meet you there, God willing. Otherwise look for us out here. Repairs can be made while we drift north."

It was agreed. They filmed Segundo serving hot coffee in wooden bowls, then shook hands before stepping back into the dory; they rowed back to the *Rigel* as if their lives depended upon it. It was Tom's turn to row. Dan held the microphone in his hand, recording—as he had been doing while on board—the sounds of the wind, the voices and the sea. At 0900 the *Rigel* pulled away, leaving us alone on the ocean. We hoisted the lateen and made for port, propelled by a favorable wind.

Landfall at Chicama

We bolted through the water like a filly let out of the barn on a spring morning. I sat in the stern with one hand on the mainsheet and the other on the sweep oar. The *Feathered Serpent*, moody and unmanageable, was now on proper course. If she could only sail like this where and when we wanted! She was steering herself, cutting through the choppy water like a fast sloop. The pressure on the sweep oar was terrific. I could not have altered the course had I wanted to. But for the moment everything was beautiful, and I couldn't help feeling a deep pride in her. Meanwhile, Segundo sat quietly on the platform deck near the stern, staring blankly into space. He was ill and perplexed. The expedition was turning out to be far more difficult than he had expected. He hadn't counted on seasickness, nor had he anticipated conditions of the sea with which he was unfamiliar.

Forty-five minutes brought us into the midst of a small fishing fleet. The golden coast drew closer and we could see the breakers shooting up the beach. Segundo hailed the skipper of a fairly small boat three points abaft the starboard beam and asked him to give us a hand. A native fisherman with copper skin and straight black hair sticking out from under a lopsided old cap waved from the green-and-white pilot house, shaking his head in recognition of our request. Pulling up alongside, one of his crewmen passed us a line. Segundo caught it and asked what port was the nearest.

"Chicama," came the answer.

Making it fast to the painter, Segundo gave the signal. Instead of pulling away at a slow, reasonable speed, the small boat dug up the water with its screw. The line broke before we had a chance to yell out. Another boat, larger than the first, came chugging up, taking the smaller one's place. Had the small boat not moved out of the way, the new boat would have plowed into it with its bow. A line was passed. Segundo took hold of it, but there was not enough rope. He motioned for more line to be payed out. Instead, the skipper put the *bolichera* in reverse. Its stern tore into the figureheads. I watched helplessly as the bowsprits widened. I heard the sickening sound of crackling bamboo and the tearing of reeds. With a snap, the port figurehead came off the bowsprit and hung crazily to one side. I could have wept.

The sea was running and confused. Dead in the water, the *Feathered Serpent* bounced around like a log. I tried to warn the skipper to start off easy and keep his speed down, but before the words could leave my mouth, I felt a lurch. The ropes grew taut. Slowly the great balsa inched forward, stubbornly, like a reluctant steer being pulled by a cowboy's lariat. The speed quickened. At ten knots the balsa went down by the head. Water churned over the bows until they were completely submerged. The totora was coming off in chunks and floating past. I stood horrified. The bamboo platform was under great strain and pressure from the foaming sea. Part of the starboard keel popped to the surface and floated away in our wake. The skipper of the *bolichera* and his crew were having a great time waving their arms about and shouting at the tops of their voices like spectators at a rodeo. Something had to be done, and fast!

"Cut the line!" I yelled. Segundo was on his way before the last word left my lips. He grabbed a machete from the deckhouse roof above the door. I went shouldering past the navigator with a pocket knife in my right hand. Struggling against the onrushing sea that swept over the bamboo deck forward, we hacked away at the manila line like men gone mad as the sea rushed through our legs. After what seemed an eternity, the line finally parted with a twang. Ten yards whipped back and nearly threw Segundo into the sea. He caught himself in the nick of time by hanging onto the starboard bowsprit. Up came the bows like a submarine surfacing with a splash of seafoam. Shaking his fist at the fleeing fishing boat, Segundo yelled out a curse. What had been a great sport for them had nearly cost us the balsa and the expedition. Too upset at the damage to say anything, we hauled the wet line aboard. Then from out of nowhere the *Rigel* appeared. They had seen the whole thing from the harbor and come to our rescue. Taking our line, they towed us to a small mooring buoy and tied us up until the harbor launch, skippered by the captain of the port, Nicolás Céspedes, puttered out to welcome us. We made fast to the jetty at 0500 hours. It had been an incredible day . . . and a near disaster.

After that harrowing experience, Segundo's attitude changed for the better. I guess he decided, in the quietness of his own soul, that a sea expedition was really no different from one on land. The 260 square feet of working deck was a small plot of ground, indeed, but it was home and had to be defended. He must have realized that the sea, like the jungle, offered dangers. The man unprepared was lost.

My heart was heavy as I surveyed the damage to the *Feathered Serpent*. The bowsprits were completely out of kilter. One figurehead was gone. Only half the starboard keel remained. (Segundo dove underneath the balsa the next day and ascertained that it was split up the middle.) We would have to make do without the whole keel, for there was no getting the balsa out of the water now. Installing another while she was afloat was out of the question. It was frozen between the expanded totora, like a wedge driven into a log.

Leaving Segundo on board with the navigator, I walked on shaky legs down the jetty toward the village. We would need additional totora, and I wanted to radio Huanchaco before Abilio left. The captain of the port promised to help us find a ship's carpenter the following morning and offered me a room with bed and shower. I gratefully accepted. There was nothing more I could have possibly wished than to be left alone. With nothing else to be done before morning, I sent word to the balsa not to expect me that night.

Outside the door a car turned the corner and came to a halt in front of me in a cloud of dust. Out stepped several members of the press corps. They had driven from Trujillo. I was utterly astonished that they had learned of our predicament so soon. The photographers wanted to know where the balsa was. I pointed in the direction of the jetty and they took off, leaving the reporters with pads and pencils in hand.

Was the expedition off? Word was around that we weren't able to sail. Was this true? If not, why were we here? I explained the problem, saying that nothing critical was wrong, that everything would be fixed in a day or so and we would continue up the coast. Satisfied, they hurried off to Trujillo to file their stories ahead of everyone else. I planned to telephone my own story with details to *El Comerico* next day.

At 2200 hours I was aroused from a deep sleep by a knocking at the door. Abilio and his crew of two men had arrived with totora, the missing daggerboard, bamboo, and other essentials. I was never so glad to see anyone in my life. I filled him in on the day's episode and he left, promising to awaken me early the next morning.

With the rising sun I rolled out of bed, showered, and started to shave, only to change my mind . . . now was the time to grow a beard. Abilio came with the Huanchaqueros to fetch me and we breakfasted together. Sipping my coca tea and munching on a piece of dry toast while the others consumed huge amounts of boiled potatoes, eggs, and pots of hot chocolate, I buried my nose in a copy of *South American Sailing Directions*. The Peruvian current, I found, was strongest at this point in its northward flow about ten miles offshore, exactly where we had drifted, out to about forty miles westward. The balsa would be facing a dual danger in the days ahead—if we managed to sail. The southward-flowing Niño current was stronger at this time of year. That meant staying out at least five miles. At Tumbez, some four hundred nautical miles to the north on the southern limits of the Gulf of Guayaquil, the Peruvian current swings westward. One arm sweeps to the Galápagos Islands, borne out by raft expeditions taken to the islands when departing from Tumbez. This danger could be avoided by not getting too far out to sea. I calculated forty to fifty miles to be the maximum distance we would safely sail offshore. Breakfast over, we collected the cargoes of totora, bamboo cane, daggerboard, and carpenter's tools that had been stored in the hotel overnight. Ten minutes of brisk walking brought us to the jetty, where we stood overlooking the *Feathered Serpent* lying comfortably at her berth on the leeside of the pier. Shouting through cupped hands, Abilio called: *"Buenos días, señores.* Hey, there, Segundo, wake up! Do you think you can sleep your way to Central America?"

Segundo stuck his head out of the entrance to the deckhouse. Nobody was going to rob him of his sleep without good reason. "Shut up out there and let a man sleep," he thundered, a scowl etched on his bearded face. When he saw Abilio his eyebrows went up six inches. *"Dios santo,* where in the world did you come from? The other side of the moon?"

"From the Pyramid of the Moon, maybe," answered Abilio, laughing. "What have you done to our beautiful balsa? Must we tend you like women?"

"Women indeed," called Segundo, now bent over the stern as he splashed sea water over his bearded face. "For sailors, you Huanchaqueros make good carpenters." He dried himself with a red towel and pulled on a pair of white slacks over his shorts. Then he came up the ramp toward us munching on a big yellow banana. It was just like old times again.

True to his word, the captain of the port sent two ship's carpenters to assist us. By sunset we had completed the job. The extra daggerboard had been attached to the sweep oar at the blade, extending its length to twenty feet. The bows were repaired, and a new figurehead replaced the broken one. We rolled up the square sail on a bamboo yard and stowed it on board in the event the lateen failed—squareriggers are downwind sailers, and the sail might give us a better chance. As for the broken daggerboard, there was absolutely nothing we could do but trust that the remaining part would be adequate to the task it was designed for.

I had made the decision to sail out of the harbor on our own in the morning. Word had spread that we were landlubbers dependent on towboats. The CBS crew had arrived the day before; rumor had it that the expedition was off, that we were unseaworthy. I read the message in their eyes. It was now or never for the *Feathered Serpent* to prove herself to these doubting Thomases. Both Segundo and the navigator agreed—I think they were as fired up as I was.

On Our Way Again

We dressed ship with all the pennants and streamers and hoisted the club burgee and Peruvian ensign. Segundo made one final attempt to get Abilio to join us, but to no avail. Taking advantage of the wind and current, we cast off from the leeside of the mole. We pivoted and, when safely away from the piles, dropped the sweep oar into the water, securing it in the thole pins. The big lateen was hoisted, and, taking the helm, I waved good-bye to our friends at Chicama. With a fresh breeze blowing from the southwest, the sail popped as it filled with wind. I put the helm over to starboard and we were off like a bolt of lightning. Our course was west-southwest, to keep us well clear of the many fishing boats at anchor in the northern mouth of the harbor. To my recollection the *Feathered Serpent* was never again to cut the water as she did that day. With a twenty-mile wind and the big lateen, she had everything going for her. We swept past the *Rigel* and the CBS crew, their mouths agape. How we got through the maze of boats I'll never know. Anyway, she sailed free as a bird, her streamers flying, a lovely thing to behold.

But we had new troubles on board. The sweep oar kept popping out of the water, and we had done all we could to force it down. It was my intention, after clearing harbor, to make a new course to the northwest. But again the *Feathered Serpent* was steering herself . . . with her crew hanging onto the sweep oar for dear life. Old-time sailors might laugh, but I felt as if we were in the grip of the roaring forties. I will never know what our speed was. Someone on the *Rigel* later estimated it to be over ten knots. We sliced through the foaming white crests that broke against the balsa from the bows. The *Feathered Serpent* rode over them like a *caballito*, then surfed down the other side at fantastic speeds.

Our point proved and the balsa well beyond the peering eyes at Chicama, I ordered the sail dropped, furled, and tied down. We lay ahull, bouncing around on the open sea like a bale of hay. Out of the corner of my eye I saw the *Rigel* far in the distance, coming to our aid. Robert Harris, a catamaran designer and one of the expedition advisers, had forewarned me of possible trouble with the sweep oar coming to the surface and had advised me to weight it down. I had the weights removed from our depth lines and the oar hauled aboard. The *Rigel* approached and heaved us a line. Segundo made it fast to the painter, and they towed us in, slowly, to keep us from drifting back to Chicama.

In the meantime an eight-pound piece of lead weight was lashed to the lower part of the oar blade. When the oar was put back into the water, it stayed down. We changed the *Feathered Serpent* to a squarerigger and downwind sailer by using the square sail in place of the lateen. With less canvas she would be much slower, but we hoped to have more control. Letting go the line from the *Rigel*, we hoisted sail. The big lateen was lashed to the side and never used again during the expedition.

With entirely new lines and a new sail set, the balsa puffed along under her own power at four or five knots. There was great excitement on board the circling *Rigel*. Our course was west; we were on our way again, with our escort following several hundred yards behind to keep an eye on us. At sunset the *Rigel* blew its foghorn to tell us it was returning to port. On Friday, April 18, our fourth day out, we waved good-bye to an old friend we were never to see again. Any sense of security we might have had while she was with us disappeared along with the fading light of day. With the moon casting a silver glow over the Pacific, we continued west under the first stars. I think we all felt our smallness.

Notes from my log the following day, Saturday, April 19, read:

0015. Have just come off watch. I am dazed from working the helm four hours. It is a real back-breaker trying to maintain a proper course. To know you are responsible for the balsa and the welfare of two other men is hardly a pleasant experience. The big sweep oar is simply too much for one man to handle. Holding it in proper position for any period of time is impossible. The sea was running, and big waves coming in from the port quarter kept slapping the oar from side to side. It seemed to bend inward two or three feet at the blade before snapping back with a bang that shook the whole raft from bow to stern. I thanked God I had selected good, strong Oregon pine for the oar. Other times the oar jumped up out of the water as we went surfing down a wave. It made a cracking sound, shuddered, and dropped back into the water. Sometimes at the crest of a big breaking wave the balsa was slewed broadside, but the sail and steering oar would bring us back on course before the next wave hit. The plunging and pounding of the balsa were terrific. The many hours that José and his master craftsmen put in lashing the bundles securely to the bamboo float with strong, well-knotted manila lines were now paying off . . .

1600. Segundo has just come off watch as tired as I was. He is concerned—and I don't blame him. How are we to work like this for another 60 days or more? I doubt if we can take it. The oar takes too much energy and saps a man. Our course continues NNW. Speed good.

2000. Have relieved the navigator. He is as bushed as we had been when coming off watch hours before. We haven't eaten much today. Segundo is too tired to cook. Both he and the navigator crunch on biscuits and drink fresh water. It's coca tea for me. Heating water on the stove isn't difficult. Am using the big two-quart metal vacuum bottle, which lasts all day. Am putting coca leaves and honey in water, which seems to satisfy my thirst and hunger. Drank a few handfuls of sea water today for thirst. Not bad-tasting. Felt much stronger afterward. Found I could swallow a little easier. This should help replace the salt loss . . . also keep down dehydration. Tried eating a fresh banana but threw it up an hour later.

2400. Segundo has come on watch. Gave him what helpful instructions I could. He was dressed in a long wool poncho to keep the cold out, and a cap pulled down over his ears.

0300. Can't sleep. My body aches. Muscles of my back and legs feel as though I had climbed a 100,000-foot mountain. Every few seconds a big swell rolls against the side of the *Feathered Serpent* with a stunning shock that sends reverberations throughout the balsa. The sound keeps me awake. I find myself waiting for them. One gets the impression the big slams are going to pound the balsa to pieces. Undercanvased and sailing before the wind, heavy with cargo and unproved, we are asking quite a bit of her. I pray she will hold up. With every shock I find myself gripping the sides of the bunk with my hands. Finally I slipped into a wool pullover sweater and felt for my deck shoes in a small netted hammock tied to the thatched roof where each of us carries the personal articles needed daily. I swung my legs over the bunk to go out on deck. They hit something. Quickly I withdrew my legs and turned on my flashlight. It was Segundo sitting in the opening aft near my head, huddled up in his poncho. What in the world is he doing there? I wondered. He should have been outside at the helm. His eyes glinted back at me like silver coins. Then he winked at me and, tugging at my sleeve, whispered for me to go out on deck, that he had solved the steering problem. This I had to see for myself. I went out on deck fearing the worst, but when I glanced at the compass we were right on course, NNW. How had he done it? The sweep oar was tied securely in place by the tiller lines; a crosspiece had been added to the oar—for easier handling, I supposed. Segundo informed me that by revolving the sweep oar with the aid of the crosspiece, much as one would turn a ratchet wheel, one could steer quite easily. He untied the lines and I found that when the oar was turned to the left or portside, the raft veered port; when turned to the right side or starboard, the raft turned right—just like the rudder on a modern vessel. It was ridiculously simple. Once the course was set, the helmsman had only to secure the position of the oar with the tiller lines, and, making an occasional correction on the crosspiece, a course was held without the great strain of moving the whole sweep oar from one side to the other. Segundo was famous for coming up with such innovations in the jungle to make things work more easily. Now he had done it at sea.

0930. The task of helmsman has been made easier by Segundo's ingenious arrangement. All aboard excited about how well it works. With the sweep oar lashed in position and the mainsheet secured, there is more time to relax on watch. Smart work on the part of Segundo, a landlubber.

1530. Earlier a large island loomed up. I took out the U. S. Pilot Chart. According to it and my own dead reckoning we had logged 112 miles since leaving port of Chicama. Not bad. Our day's run had averaged a respectable four knots. including the previous four hours. Far better than I had hoped for. The island appears to be Lobos de Afuera. If it is, we will have to alter course. The fact that we were west of the island leaves me in consternation: the navigator had plotted a course earlier in the day and said the island was still west of us. José had warned us to stay between the larger Lobos de Afuera and the smaller Lobos de Tierra. Our position exceeds the 40-mile limit I had made. We are in danger of being caught in the westward-moving current that flows to the Pacific Islands. When I explained this to Segundo he was infuriated. He never did like the idea of staying out of sight of land. The navigator tends to want to stay well out to sea. . . .

Segundo wants to drop the sail or come about and head for land, where he can keep an eye on things. I am still not certain about the navigator's skill and am of the opinion only time will tell. I asked Segundo to hold off until we are absolutely certain of our position. Taking out my binoculars, I began to examine the island.

1540. Fishing boat of excited native fishermen chugs up. They hail from the port of San José de Lambayeque. Evidently they haven't heard of the expedition. The crewmen run back and forth on the deck waving their arms over their heads and shouting. I can well imagine their shock at seeing a huge totora balsa bearing down upon them from the open sea. We are in the waters of the great King Naylamp, whose fleet of sailing balsas landed on these shores centuries ago. Lambayeque is strewn with ancient remains, and museums of the world contain gorgeous ceramics and other artifacts taken from the treasure cities of Lambayeque, Etén, and others. Perhaps they think we are King Naylamp and his attendants. I wonder what tales they will recount to the townspeople when returning to port. Segundo hails them and asks the name of the island. "Lobos de Afuera," comes the reply. With this they chug off just as quickly as they had come. Segundo and I are both disturbed by the navigator's error. It is important that we work in concert, however. I casually recommend that he alter course, which he does. I do not check it, because I want to bolster his confidence.

2000. Rested most of day. Some photography. Seas calm, light breeze from SE. Caught up on notes and log. Taped sounds of splashing sea against bow on tape recorder. All quiet. Segundo calmer.

April 20th, 6th day out.

0230. During graveyard watch, Segundo woke us. A fishing boat attracted to our running lights had stopped by for a chat. When I came out on deck the crew was chatting with Segundo, who held a pair of large bonitos in his hands, a gift from the captain. We gave them some cans of fruit (Segundo still eager to lighten balsa). Sea much calmer. Speed has slowed. The night is beautiful. The stars wink at us in an endless wheeling arc as has been observed by sailors for countless centuries. Fishing boat steams off, leaving us alone.

0500. Navigator informs us that a cachalot is circling the boat. We keep our voices down to a whisper. None of us has gotten a good look at the whale, but we can hear it blowing and splashing its tail. The navigator thinks it is a baby. We strain our eyes for a glimpse of it, to no avail. It finally moves away, deciding, to our vast relief, not to give us a nudge—or take a chunk out of us like a cow chewing at a haystack.

0900. For the second time this morning a fishing boat drops in for a visit. It is followed by a companion moments later. The crew of the first one excitedly tells us our present course will take us between the island of Lobos de Tierra and the shore. When I came on watch, the balsa's heading was NNW, which was too northward for my liking, and I quickly altered it to a bearing of true west on the compass in order to compensate for the magnetic variation. Our position is bad news. José warned of the strong currents in the channel between Lobos de Tierra and Cabo Verde that can—and have—driven boats on shore. Now the fishermen are telling us to get farther out to sea. How have we come so close to shore, now an estimated 10 miles to the east? There are only three possibilities: (1) the navigator's bearing was too far north; (2) the strong currents have pulled us east; and (3) the onshore winds during the night have blown us eastward.

0925. The wind telltale of flagged line hanging on either side of the crossarms at the mastheads hangs straight down. No wind. Currents strong. The *Feathered Serpent* starts hobby-horsing in the riverlike currents, and I can see we are drifting toward shore some seven miles to the east. We are nearly becalmed. The Niño current appears to be working against us. If we cannot get past the island, we are in grave peril.

1020. Island is much larger than Lobos de Afuera. I estimate it to be about 7 miles long by 3 miles wide. Wind has increased and is carrying us NW. Currents have weakened and the *Feathered Serpent* is sailing slowly along. We are confident.

By two o'clock in the afternoon we rounded the island at midchannel. We logged fifteen miles at an average speed of three knots since sighting it at 0900. We were about three miles from the island and a little less than four miles from Cabo Verde. Too close for comfort. Our zigzag course through the tidal currents and the southward-flowing Niño current indicates these forces will have to be reckoned with in the future. We will have to use the offshore winds that blow out to sea during the day to get far enough out (but never beyond the forty-mile limit) to counter the onshore winds that have a tendency to pull us to the coast at night. Segundo, more confident with shore in sight, has yet to understand the danger of getting too close to land.

"It is going to be a troublesome voyage," said Segundo with an unaccustomed air of detachment. He was at the helm, stretched out on the bamboo deck, wearing a pair of khaki pants cut off at the thighs. He wore a huge straw hat pulled down over his eyes. He was tending the sweep oar with his left foot as nonchalantly as if he were riding a mule. Occasionally he lifted his head to look at the shoreline or take a compass reading. Otherwise he was totally relaxed and enjoying himself. "Very troublesome," he repeated.

The navigator was taking a sun shot at the bow, leaving Segundo and me alone at the helm. With the danger now seemingly past, everyone was less tense. We were perfectly content to let the wind and current do the work, the main objective being to get as far west as possible while staying out of trouble. I wasn't paying too much attention to Segundo's words, busying myself with cleaning my camera lenses.

"I think I'll get off at the next port," he said, sitting up to take a compass reading. "I don't belong here."

"What's that you say?" I asked almost casually, not wanting to reveal the anxiety his words had caused me. I not only needed his help, but didn't want to go on without my trusted old friend. What upset me was the calmness with which he spoke: that meant he had already given some thought to leaving. But perhaps he had not made a firm decision: I still might be able to cajole him into staying.

"I want to go home," he said.

"Why?" I asked.

He didn't answer. And nothing more was said about it for several days.

The navigator returned to tell me our compass required calibrating. According to him it was off some 20 degrees. The chronometer was running several minutes behind. He advised that we make port immediately. Segundo looked at me sideways. Nevertheless, I observed that he seemed to cheer up at the mention of putting in. Other repairs and replacements had to be made. And I could think of a dozen small items that could make life easier on board. So, making port was not such a bad idea, after all. We had no idea of when this would be, but the thought perked us all up. I was heartened by Segundo's change of attitude. Maybe he would stick it out. Punta Negra lay thirty miles northwest of us. By sailing another ten miles beyond this point we could then veer due north. I for one would feel much better with Punta Negra behind us.

I had no inkling of what lay ahead.

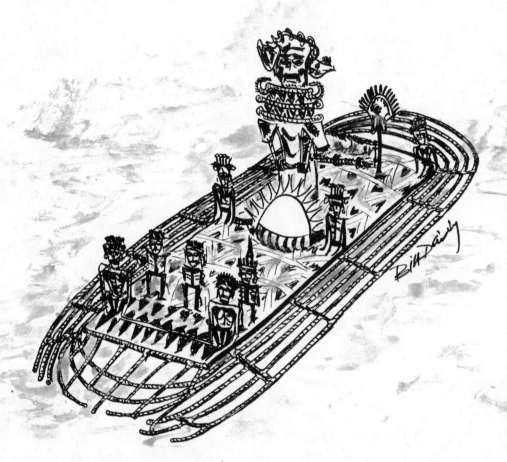

Muisca votive raft with El Dorado figure. Drawn by Bill K. Dailey from original on display in the Museo del Oro, Bogotá, Colombia.

———— ◆ ————

Escape from the Breakers

Days before, a little guanay bird attached itself to the starboard bowsprit. Sometimes it would flap aboard and pick around the pots and pans, making itself quite at home. It appeared content to ride along with us, observing our routine with disdain. Every so often I would catch it peering at me with an indifferent gaze. With a canned sardine, I once got my hand to within a few inches of its head. Fresh anchovy was its fare, I imagined, for it paid no more attention to my peace offering than it had to our old soup. Finally it spotted a fishing boat several hundred yards behind our stern and took off, skipping along above the water to join a mixed company of sea birds feeding on scraps of fresh bait thrown overboard. We waited for its return but never saw it again. I hoped its going wasn't a bad omen. Shortly after the exit of our feathered visitor, we caught sight of a swordfish surfacing out of the water to salute the rising sun, its dark purple body reflecting the early morning light before plunging gracefully back into the sea. What wouldn't the fishermen of Cabo Blanco give to hook such a sea monster, I thought. It must have weighed 1,500 pounds. Not many like this are to be seen around these parts since the big fish disappeared a few years before, much to the chagrin of sport fishermen who flocked from all parts of the world to try their luck. Later in the day I recorded in the expedition's log:

Monday, April 21, 7th day out.

0845. Filling dropped out of one of my molars last night right after I observed a tuna clipper through binoculars. Have filled up the cavity with chewing gum. Seems to work. No pain, except when gum drops out.

1000. A school of dolphins surfaced off the port beam. I watched them sporting about, the males blowing like bulls in the arena.

1630. The clatter of an approaching airplane broke the monotonous sounds of the sea, the wind and the spray, and the creaking of the balsa. The navigator was at the helm, Segundo was taking a well-deserved rest at the bows. I had been filming, and when the first sound came to my ears I dashed into the deckhouse to fetch the walkie-talkie. A CBS plane was due and its presence thrilled us. It circled once, then dove and zoomed the balsa. This was repeated until I got the walkie-talkie going. Tom Spain's voice crackled over the air. "Hello, Ku-Vi-Qu, hello, Ku-Vi-Qu." I answered excitedly after contact had been made, and, small talk out of the way, we were told that we were reported sinking last light. A fishing boat had radioed the news. I conjectured it was the *bolichera* that we had met in the straits between Lobos de Tierra and Cabo Verde. Evidently they feared we would never get through the currents—quite justifiably, I suppose, considering that the currents are so strong that light-powered fishing boats can have difficulty making headway against them.

　　We chatted back and forth, then made ourselves look busy filming as the small plane cruised above. With one final zoom and a farewell click of the walkie-talkie, the plane faded away to the northwest, promising to return on the morrow.

1700. Opened the sail bags and inspected extra sails. They all appeared in good shape, being dry. Shot 200 feet of movie film along with an hour of recording tape. Beautiful sunset. Wind subsides and we are nearly becalmed toward sunset. Expect to round Punta Negra sometime during night, though we plan to keep sailing west until daylight to avoid getting too close to shore.

Next day found us caught in a flat calm that lasted two days. The sail hung flat and the sky was overcast. Quite a dreary situation it was. We drifted lazily along, propelled by the current, not knowing our exact position or where we were going, but praying it was north and not west. The navigator was unable to shoot the sun with his sextant.

A little after noon we ran into a school of tuna. The sea was literally alive with their thrashing silvery-blue bodies. It was as if we could get out and walk on them. They were everywhere. I never imagined there could be so many fish in one place. Segundo baited several hooks, threw them overboard, then grabbed the big fishing net hanging on the deckhouse and ran to the stern. Using his toes, he secured himself against the starboard bowsprit where he tried to catch one of the tuna as they came flying out of the water. When this failed, he took the gaff and, like a baseball player taking swipes at a curve ball, lunged for the tuna, also without result. This continued for several hours—good sport for Segundo and fun to watch—until he was completely tuckered out. Then, at four o'clock in the afternoon, an eight-pound tuna took a hook thrown over the starboard stern. Segundo hauled him in carefully and threw a net over the bonito, then ran to the galley for garlic, onions, vinegar, chili, pepper and salt. Once Segundo got the hang of it, the cooking pot was always filled with fish stew.

From the Log

Wednesday, April 23, 9th day out.

1030. Sighted land. This confirms our northerly course. Navigator made a sextant observation and reported our position to be off Talara. Sea calm. *Feathered Serpent* continues to pulse along with the currents. Course varies 40 to 60 degrees on compass (NE) to carry us around Cabo Blanco.

1100. Strong wind from SE. Sail fills with wind. New sextant reading puts us off coast of Paita, 50 nautical miles south of our estimated position half an hour earlier. Navigator says currents are pushing us south.

1500. New sextant observation. Our position is just south of Talara. Navigator predicts we will reach Cabo Blanco tomorrow. I alter course to get us farther out to sea before evening onshore winds begin to blow.

1515. Sea fairly calm, little wind. We are not within sight of land. I decide to see how the *Feathered Serpent* looks from a distance and to give her a general inspection. I elect to try out one of the *caballitos*, something I have always wanted to do. The lines, made tight by sea water, give me some difficulty. Segundo is at the helm and rightfully should remain there. He observes me struggling with the knots for several minutes, then, apparently having lost patience, comes over and cuts them with a swipe of his pocket knife, picks up the *caballito* and throws it into the sea, putting its mooring line in my hands with a grunt before returning to the sweep oar. The *Feathered Serpent* is self-contained and we carry everything we need for several weeks at sea. Still, I like to preserve even the smallest bit of line, since it cannot be replaced if we fail to make port again.

I jump into the sea with nothing but a pair of shorts between me and the sharks that my imagination tells me are swimming just beneath the water. Pushing the truncated end with my hands dog-paddle fashion, I move several yards away from the larger balsa. The next step is to mount the cigar-shaped totora float and paddle around the *Feathered Serpent*. Little do I realize the practice required to handle one of these corklike floats. Every time I pull myself up into position to throw a leg over, the float simply rolls over. I feel as if I am in a rodeo trying to stay mounted on a Brahma bull for ten seconds. I finish out of the money, swallow my pride, and swim 50 yards away from the *Feathered Serpent*. The same current that pushes the larger balsa carries the smaller *caballito* along with it, so there is no danger of becoming separated. As a precaution, a cord around my wrist connects me to the *caballito*.

The balsa is a beautiful sight observed from a distance, even with her sail and pennants slack. She sways on the surface of the sea like a grandmother in a rocking chair, as content as if she were on her own front porch relaxing in the afternoon shade. It gives me a strange feeling to watch the men on the balsa going about their daily routine. It is almost like watching a movie with me as the spectator, not the participant. Segundo has climbed the Jacob's ladder, keeping a sharp lookout for land. The navigator occupies himself coiling up a length of line at the bows. Segundo is scurrying down the rope ladder and scampering back to the helm. The sails billow out, a wind has come up. I lose no time in kicking the *caballito* and myself back to the balsa. Approaching the portside of the bamboo deck, I am about to pull myself up and the *caballito* after me when I notice a few gooseneck barnacles along the waterline. I dive under for a better look. I suppose there are several hundred of the tiny crustaceans clinging to the bottom of the float. I swim over to starboard side and find the same thing. There aren't enough to actually slow us up. I am more worried about the big chunk missing from the daggerboard. I swim casually to the portside, and as I try to pull myself up on deck, a big wave comes out of nowhere and dashes me up against the bamboo gunwale. One of the canes jams into my ribcage. I feel a dull pain in my lower right side but think nothing of it until I try to haul myself up on deck. The effort hurts so much that I have to slip back down into the water. When I take a deep breath the pain is even worse, and I discover I cannot yell for help. Fortunately, Segundo has been keeping an eye on me and helps me on deck and back to the deckhouse. Then he secures the *caballito* and returns to the helm.

2200. The *Feathered Serpent* is gusting along in the right direction. According to my dead reckoning we should pass Paita during the night or early morning and reach Talara within 48 hours. Earlier I was depressed, partly because of my aching ribs (which I have taped up) and partly because of my weakness. But I am feeling better after having drunk a cup of coca tea and several mouthfuls of seawater.

2330. All three running lights went out, and the moon ducked behind a dark cloud mass. Suddenly I was enveloped in

(Left) *Native shipwright from Huanchaco, Peru.* (Top right) *Huanchaqueros binding totora-reed bundles to form floats.* (Bottom right) *Bamboo poles to be used for deck.*

The author and José Arzola-Huamanchumo, head shipwright, inspect floats before bamboo deck is lashed in place. Salaverry, Peru. *(UPI photo.)*

(Left) *Crane lifting reed float at the marina in Salaverry.* (Center) *The* Feathered Serpent *floats high and dry. Decking, deckhouse and rigging have not been lashed into place.* (Bottom left) *Deck has been lashed on floats; framework for deckhouse is going up. Note centerboards in the form of serpent heads.* (Right) *The author with CBS newsman Charles Kuralt. (Photo by Tom Spain, CBS News.)*

The lateen sail painted with Indian designs is hoisted, and the test begins.

(Opposite) *Tugboat* Sala-verry *drops towline one mile from breakwater of Salaverry, and the* Feath-ered Serpent *begins its long journey. (Photo by Malcolm Burke.)*

(Right) *Segundo cleaning the day's catch at the stern.*

(Opposite) *Romping along.*

(Right) *Ecuadorian sailboat pulls alongside with a gift of fish.*

A curious shark snoops around looking for a handout.

Banners flying, the sail filled with wind and the sun setting on the sea, the Feathered Serpent *scampers toward Manta.*

Segundo fights off the shark.

Shark on board.

The bowsprit figureheads preside over the foaming sea.

Sail furled, the Feathered Serpent drifts aong with the current.

darkness. There was no sense in trying to relight the lamps. They simply wouldn't work. I think sea water got inside the fuel container. After my eyes became adjusted to the darkness, I noticed for the first time that the *Feathered Serpent* was enveloped in a pale white light. She appeared to be aglow. The sea was phosphorescent, as though a thousand beacon lights were being sent up from the bottom of the sea, imprisoning the balsa in a cone of light within a diameter of 600 feet. At the bows, under the serpent figureheads, an undulating mass of glittering white built up into great masses of foamy froth that streaked along the sides of the balsa, leaving a trail of diamondlike phosphorescence, like a shooting star. The glow was under my feet as it swirled about the floats and splashed through the bamboo deck. Even the sweep oar was radiant, like the hand of a giant clock. I felt like an astronaut flying through space.

2350. Close to midnight the wind rose and the *Feathered Serpent* took wing. Sheets of phosphorescent foam flew past as the balsa began to run with the wind, her totora creaking. The heading was downwind to a 25-knot wind.

2420. Segundo has relieved me at the helm. The *Feathered Serpent* starts slamming as she labors through the heavy seas. She will take a terrible pounding before the night is over. We alter course to 40 degrees NE in order to ride along with the big slams breaking in from aft. This cuts down some of the punishment she is forced to take. We estimate we are about 35 miles from land, far enough to allow the new course without risk of running aground, for the navigator states firmly we are near Cabo Blanco and should round it within a few hours. According to my calculations we are farther south—at least a good day's run away. The navigator is afraid we will be pulled out to sea by the south equatorial current and wants to draw closer to shore. On this point Segundo is, of course, in agreement. I am afraid of the inshore current and warn them to stay alert. In any event we should know our position come morning.

Breakers Ahead

Late morning on April 24, our tenth day out, we rounded a land mass which I took to be Foca Point. Our position was latitude 5° 50′ south, longitude 81° 40′ west, according to my dead reckoning. The navigator took several sun sights with the sextant, went indoors and worked out our position. When he came out an hour later he announced triumphantly in nasal tones that the point was in fact Cabo Blanco, and that from now on it would be easy sailing. His estimated position was a good 65 miles north of where I thought we were. Earlier, Segundo and I had sighted an island that answered the description of Foca Island. With the aid of my binoculars and Segundo's excellent vision (as powerful as my own 9x35 lenses) we took a reading on a 3,740-foot peak to the northeast with my hand bearing compass. The navigator, who took a reading on a smaller mountain to the south, had made a blunder. I found it difficult to account for his error. I noticed he used a set of hydrographic charts compiled by Matthew Maury, an American naval oceanographer who made a survey of the west coast of South America around 1840. I knew from the old tuna-boat skippers that the mountains were not accurately placed on charts and that an error of twenty miles or more is possible. But this would not account for an error of 65 miles. Later, when he took a noon position, it did not agree with the bearings taken on the mountain peak earlier. He failed to take an ex-meridian altitude of the sun to find our proper latitude. It appeared to me that the navigator had not had enough experience to maintain a proper balance of the sextant bubble, perhaps due to our bouncing balsa. Probably he could have navigated on a larger vessel with ease. It takes special training to navigate on a small craft. I cursed myself for being lazy and not taking a course on celestial navigation as I had planned, and swore never again to let anyone do my navigating for me. As it was, I instructed the navigator to make a very careful check on his sightings and to plot our course as best he could.

The wind was still dead behind us from the southwest. We were not doing nearly so well as we had before sighting Lobos de Tierra. We had moved approximately 120 miles up the coast during a 96-hour period for an average of a little more than one knot (we probably logged much more, since our course was erratic). The night's run had brought us closer to shore—some five miles off—which comforted Segundo but worried me to some degree because of the inshore currents in the vicinity.

When the sun lowered into the ocean, we sighted a port and hoisted the Peruvian ensign and the red-and-white pennants. We wanted very much to attract the attention of some fishing boats to check our position, and possibly make port. We dropped sail, but the current pushed us along past the fading lights.

The wind coming from the southwest shortly afterward was good news, and we hoisted the sail again and galloped along on a northwesterly course, logging 38 miles during the next 11 hours for an average speed of 4 knots. We got the running lights working again, and I prayed we would run into a fishing fleet here on the inside of the Continental Shelf. We kept a sharp lookout and tried to bear out to sea, as we were too near the land for peace of mind. We could have sailed closer to the wind with the lateen sail but were afraid of using it. The squarerigger was doing its job. We were not experienced enough with the lateen. The *Feathered Serpent* was slamming badly, and I was afraid she would be set aback. The sweep oar was difficult to handle in the high seas, and all three of us stood watch until 2100 hours, when the wind fell off suddenly and I sent Segundo and the navigator in to rest.

When I went off watch at midnight I could hear the rollers breaking on the beach. I figured we were no more than three miles offshore. The wind had dropped, and the *Feathered Serpent* was becalmed. This was a dangerous situation because of the southerly current close inshore in these waters (assuming we were in the vicinity of Talara), and the ocean swells that roll in toward the open beach at speeds of 12 to 15 knots, according to the charts. A sailboat of any kind caught in the breakers is in a hazardous situation to be avoided at all costs. Since we had no other propulsion but the wind there was nothing to do but pray. I cautioned Segundo to keep his eyes open and call me if we got in too close to shore. Then I went inside for some rest.

I slept fitfully. At 0100 I peeped outside to find Segundo at the helm. He was taking his work seriously now. The situation hadn't changed much, and I could still hear the surf breaking gently on the distant shore. There was no wind. I thought of moving the sweep oar back and forth to give us some forward motion, but we would have soon tired of pushing the great weight of the balsa, and our gain would have been infinitesimal against the force of the current. I went back inside, hating the night and the shore—and the calm. At 0300 Segundo entered the deckhouse in a state of great nervousness, shouting that we were getting close to shore. Opening my sleepy eyes, I became instantly aware of the roaring of the sea. It was terrifying. I leaped from my bunk and went out on deck in a frenzy. What I saw turned my blood to ice. The open beach was but a few yards away. The *Feathered Serpent* was precariously close to being caught in the big, breaking trochoidal waves rolling down on the beach at a velocity of 15 to 18 knots. The sound was deafening. I swore at myself for not having heard it before. A sinking feeling came over me as I imagined our beautiful craft breaking up on the beach. I guessed the deep-water waves were coming from a storm somewhere at sea. The interval between them was around twelve seconds. There wasn't much time to act. Once the waves got hold of us, no power on earth could get us away from the pulling force of so many tons of water.

"Why didn't you call me earlier?" I shouted above the din.

"It happened too fast. We were out to sea one moment, here the next. What are we going to do?"

In spite of the fact that so much depended on a quick decision, I stood transfixed, staring at the waves breaking against the bar and shooting up the beach like foamy fingers of white death. The balsa was stable, buoyant and strong, and I figured she might make it through the breakers. How to get her off the beach was another matter. As it was, we had no propulsion of any kind without the wind. The sweep oar, which, unlike the rudder, would not break up once she hit the beach, gave us no steering power at all. I thought of pouring our vegetable oil on the sea. The waves might not be stopped from breaking, but it could calm the sea and help us make a smoother landing on the beach. Then my thoughts turned to the safety of the men. I dashed into the deckhouse, shaking the navigator's shoulder with one hand and grabbing the life preservers off the wall with the other.

"What's the matter?" he asked in a guttural voice filled with sleep. I could hardly hear him.

"Wake up, man! We're about to go on the beach!" I yelled, throwing one of the vest-type life jackets on the floor near his head (he always bedded down on the floor because of his large frame). "Wake up!" Then I ran out the rear of the deckhouse and gave Segundo his life jacket while putting mine on. A quick glance at the beach showed us even closer than before. "Where is the navigator?" I yelled. Segundo shrugged his shoulders and looked wide-eyed at the beach.

Once again I dashed back inside, only to find him fast asleep. I shouted his name and told him to get up, as we were going on the beach. That seemed to stir him. Stumbling out on deck, I felt the deck fall out from under my feet as the balsa was caught in the forward face of a swell. I held my breath as we went surfing down the rolling wave. We had heaved as we rode over the crest, and I was afraid we would swing broadside or somersault. If that happened it would be the end. The waves towered nearly fifteen feet, and the troughs were about equal in depth. There was a thousand feet between each crest. Fortunately, the sweep oar held us steady. We were still out beyond the breaking cycloidal waves. If we got into those—which could be soon—we were goners.

The navigator staggered out on deck carrying his life jacket. He looked around, gasped, then turned in the direction of the helm, demanding to know who got the balsa into this mess. Segundo's face paled and his knuckles turned white as they gripped the steering oar. He alone was making the only practical contribution to the welfare of the balsa at the moment, and I think he knew it. Suddenly he stood and reached for his machete, which was tied to the thole pins. Letting out a terrible roar, he threw it into the sea. Going forward, the navigator dug out two canvas sea anchors. He brought the cone-shaped receptacles back to the stern and dumped them at Segundo's feet. "Help me with the lines," he called out. Segundo shot a quick glance in my direction. He stood there seething with rage, his face gaunt, his lips tight.

"Hold there!" I shouted.

"These will keep us off the beach," came the reply. "Give

me a hand." Then he started to disentangle the knotted lines as if he had all the time in the world. I don't know what his idea was. If thrown over the balsa at the bows, the lines would surely have floated along with us. Ordinarily a drogue was a good idea and would give a breaking effect, but no sea anchor could hold us once we got into the big breaking waves—and they were seconds away. Had we a motor it might have been different. With no wind, we were dead in the water. As I stood there, furious at our predicament and frustrated at being unable to do anything, I felt a wisp of breeze on my face. I looked up at the sail and saw it flutter. The offshore breeze was beginning to blow. Whether by luck or act of God, I did not know. But the wind was blowing.

"The wind!" I yelled out at the top of my lungs. "The wind!"

I sprang forward along the starboard side of the working platform, nearly falling into the sea when the balsa swayed as she began to climb the face of a roller. Another five hundred feet and we would be at the crest. Segundo leaped for the sweep oar, tore at the lines to free them, and put his weight against the wooden sweep, throwing it slowly to hard aport, the object being to swing the stern around and point our bows out to sea in order to take advantage of the wind. The navigator was still fiddling with the towline attached to the sea drogue. I remember yelling at him to help me with the sail.

The pain in my ribs was forgotten as I set the tack. I was running to the other side to take the clew when the navigator appeared. I put the clew in his hands and ran back to help Segundo with the sweep oar. Together we worked the oar back and forth to give us some forward motion, our eyes glued on the sail. Slowly the wind grew in intensity and the sail began to fill. I grabbed the mainsheet with my hands and let go a few feet. I secured it; then, taking the braces in both hands, I worked the yard around, to catch every puff of wind, as gently as a jockey would hold the reins of a race horse on the home stretch.

If I allowed the wind to slip out, the race was over. Suddenly the sail billowed out. Segundo kept working the oar back and forth; the stern was now facing the land and our bows pointing to sea. The wind was dead behind us from the northeast and growing in force. I glanced over my left shoulder. The crest was but a few seconds away. The color of the sea had changed from blue to green and now to muddy brown. I prayed the balsa would gain enough speed to escape the white breaker astern. If we hit the crest we would lose all control.

The *Feathered Serpent* hung in a state of suspended motion, going neither forward nor backward. Caught in the undertow and assisted by the wind, we were holding our own against the advancing rush of the wave. I held my breath and felt my heart pumping like a piston. My throat was dry, my hands sweaty. Now the *Feathered Serpent* was fighting for her life. For the first time I began to look on the balsa as a living thing rather than an inanimate hunk of reeds, bamboo, and lines. I understood how old sailors loved their ships like women and talked to them as if they had souls. I could feel the force of the sea and the wind pulsing through her structure like blood pumping through arteries . . . she was struggling to carry us away from the beach and out to sea again.

"Come, my beauty!" I shouted against the sound of the pounding surf. "Get us out of here!"

"*Vamos*, Ku-Vi-Qu," chimed in Segundo, calling the balsa by its public name. "*Vamos, vamos por Dios.*" He worked the oar rhythmically in great sweeps, giving it some momentum while gazing up at the sail. "*Sopla, viento, sopla!*" he cried. We started chanting together, "Blow, wind, blow. Blow, wind, blow."

Slowly at first, then gaining momentum, the *Feathered Serpent* pulsed ahead toward the sea. Perhaps we were going to make it after all. I prayed to God to let us escape. Remembering the Biblical account of Lot's wife, I never once looked back. The waves had been coming in groups of three, and we had successfully negotiated the last and largest sea. This gave us a chance to get outside the bar before the next series advanced upon us. We ran through, making for the open sea. We sailed carefully, avoiding the faces of the breakers, looking for dark water. We sailed along the shore, with the rumbling waves breaking against the cliffs that had replaced the open beach. I think I shall remember with terror the sound of the roaring breakers the rest of my life.

Next, we found ourselves surrounded by lights. Whether buoys or what, I could not tell. It was utterly fascinating to see so many bright lights. Once I could have sworn we were inside a harbor surrounded by the lights of the jetty. This kept up until 0400, when the navigator took over the helm. I sent Segundo in to rest. It was imperative that we conserve our strength for another crisis should it strike again. We were dangerously close to shore as it was. For the life of me I could not figure out what the strange lights were. It was uncanny. I screwed up my eyes and peered into the coal-black darkness with the aid of my glasses, to no avail. We had the disadvantage of being strangers and totally ignorant of the area. Then I went inside and lay down. At 0500 we were both up again and on deck, the drumming sound of the breakers pounding in our ears as the sea churned about us.

As dawn approached, the sun turned the reeds a bright yellow, as if they had been spun from golden straw, and hope stirred in our hearts.

Talara

We found ourselves at the entrance of a large harbor. Numerous sailboats milled about, their white sails glinting in the morning sun. I was curious to know our position. Taking out my glasses, I focused on a sail bearing down on us. It was a small raft of balsawood, steered by a single operator standing barefoot at the stern, controlling the sailing balance of the raft by a simple adjustment of the centerboard's height. I was amazed at the speed with which the flimsy craft bore down upon us. I recognized it as a sailing raft from Sechura by the botalonspar sticking out from the single mast and running to the luff of the sail. Unless I missed my guess, Talara wasn't far away. The raft cruised past off the starboard beam with a grace that made me envious. The native waterman waved and came back for a second tour of inspection before sailing off for the day's fishing, like a surfrider looking for the perfect wave. It was no good trying to call out to him because of the sound of the wind and the white crests breaking on the sea. I followed him for some time with my binoculars before sweeping the horizon. It was then that the mysterious source of the light became clear. We were virtually surrounded by offshore oil-drilling rigs.

The navigator was gazing in the same general direction at the rigs. His face was expressionless, and when he saw me looking at him he said, "The current pulled us south thirty miles." At this time a fishing boat puttered up astern and hailed us. Segundo cupped his hands and asked the name of the port. "Talara," came the reply. While we might have made it into the harbor under our own power—there was a fresh breeze blowing from the southwest—we decided to take a line. The skipper agreed to tow us to a mooring buoy in the harbor. We tidied up the balsa, then shaved and trimmed our beards.

At 0900 on our second Friday at sea, the eleventh day of our voyage, we made port at Talara, some 350 miles north of Salaverry. We had logged 86 miles per day while actually under sail, excluding the 46-hour layover at the port of Chicama.

This wasn't bad, considering the calamities that had befallen us on the way. All in all, I was quite pleased with our passage. For a drift-type vessel we could feel proud. Of course the real test lay ahead. Could we round Cabo Blanco without being pulled to the Galápagos or the South Pacific by the Humboldt current?

It was hard to believe that, only six hours before, we were fighting to save the *Feathered Serpent* from certain disaster. It was all like a bad dream that, while still vivid in our minds, had passed out of our lives with the coming day. I hoped never to have to live through anything like it again. At the moment we couldn't have been happier. The balsa was safely at anchor, we were alive and well, and the town seemed to be ours for the taking. A motor launch came alongside and took us in tow and we moored near the wharf. A military guard was put on the balsa and we were free for the night. After checking into a good hotel that assured plenty of hot water for bathing, we tromped to the nearest restaurant, where we ordered up the largest assortment of food ever put on a table. There were baskets of tropical food—bananas, papaya, oranges, granadillas, pineapple, mangoes, and avocados; dozens of French rolls with fresh butter; a huge pitcher of lemonade, big black olives and olive oil. Next came giant shrimps prepared in lemon juice and seasoned with chili, followed by baked swordfish steaks, sea bass, lobster thermidor served with potatoes of all colors and sizes—white, yellow and purple—some boiled and garnished with a peanut sauce; some mashed and rolled into large balls and stuffed with little wild birds, olives, and onions; still others fried a golden brown. There were platters of white rice covered with a special sauce of chicken and tomatoes; bowls of red beans with garlic cloves; baked green peppers stuffed with rice and tomatoes that melted in the mouth; and, for dessert, huge *chirimoya* whose delicious white meat tasted like vanilla ice cream, followed by café espresso. It was a meal fit for a king, and everyone ate heartily. I didn't keep much down but I enjoyed everything I ate at the time.

Next morning a local dentist put a temporary filling in my molar, and I had my ribs taped; one had a slight fracture, and the muscles were bruised. After that we purchased badly needed stores and gear. We found a sailmaker to make alterations on the two emergency nylon sails, which being lateen, had to be sewed together to form a single square sail to fit the yard. We also painted the missing sunburst on the canvas sail. I looked up a local blacksmith and gave him a design for a kedge anchor. I hadn't wanted to use a metal anchor (stones attached to lines were what ancients used), but after the near disaster in the breakers south of Talara, I thought better of it. In the event we went aground, a kedge would help us free the balsa. It was a simple anchor with three arms and small flukes with sharp bills to bite into any rocky bottom.

In the meantime, Segundo had shifted the weight farther astern to balance the balsa. The navigator had the instruments checked and found the chronometer to be off several minutes, which he said accounted for the navigational error he now admitted to. The captain of the port did not accept his drift story and told him so. Still, I saw no need to make an issue of the affair. The port authority checked the radio, found and replaced a burned-out fuse.

Word came in that Tom Spain of CBS had spent seventeen hours marooned in the desert when his plane ran out of gasoline and was forced down, which accounted for his not showing up April 23. They had exceeded their flight time by searching for us and hanging around too long taking pictures. When the plane failed to make an appearance at its field, it was eventually reported missing, and the papers were full of it. Spain was picked up by Peruvian authorities and held for questioning: Taking aerial photographs of Peruvian territory was prohibited. Spain was later released, but his film was confiscated, with the promise it would be returned after the inspectors had had a chance to examine it. As it turned out, the film was never recovered and Spain lost some of his best footage of the expedition. Permission to make a return flight was not granted.

Late in the afternoon Segundo again brought up the question of going home. He said he was not making a contribution to the expedition and felt bad about our being caught in the breakers. I assured him that he was needed, that he was not to blame, and that I would not think of going on without him. While he was on salary from the club, he had volunteered his services at no extra pay, wanting only the opportunity of participating in the great adventure. In this respect, both he and the navigator earned my appreciation and admiration. I offered him a bonus if he would continue, and he accepted. Later on the navigator apologized for his behavior and assured Segundo that his participation was vital to the voyage. With this problem out of the way, I turned to other important matters.

Barnacles in ever multiplying numbers had formed on the floats since we had anchored in Talara. They now covered the two floats by the thousands, like beans with sprouts, and would unquestionably slow us up. It was essential, then, that we depart at the very earliest opportunity, before the condition worsened. Had it been possible to roll the balsa up on the beach and rid it of the unwelcome guests I would have done so, but since time was against us, the next best thing was to clear port. When I explained this to the captain of the port he was most sympathetic and gave us permission to leave the following morning.

Everything looked bright until I picked up copies of the afternoon edition of the press. I was astounded to read the following in red-ink-banner headline, covering half a page:

CAPTURE OF BALSA KU-VI-QU ORDERED!

Above that ran the subhead:

ACCUSED OF TRANSPORTING ANTIQUITIES.
PERUVIAN INVESTIGATIVE POLICE ORDERED
TO INSPECT CARGO

I could hardly believe my eyes. As I read further, the text, translated from the Spanish, read:

> The balsa Ku-Vi-Qu, skippered by Gene Savoy, has been accused of transporting Peruvian antiquities of incalculable value. This accusation was made to the Peruvian Investigative Police (PIP), and Chief Inspector Hercules Marthans has ordered an inspection. He told the press that "As soon as it reaches port, it will be boarded to check the authenticity of the complaint, and if it evades Peruvian police action, IN-TERPOL will intervene." It is known that the totora balsa Ku-Vi-Qu is undertaking a voyage from Peru to Mexico with the object of proving that ancient Peruvians could have made such trips in similar fragile vessels. The fact is that the expedition is carrying utensils, ornaments, and ceramic objects, among other valuables, which are not authorized cargo since they consist of antiquities of the nation.
>
> (According to Fabian Aparcana, EXTRA)

Fearing that the balsa would be placed in legal custody and a long delay would result, I dashed outside and leaped into a cab, instructing the driver to take me to the port authority as fast as he could. I was relieved when the secretary told me that the captain of the port was in and that I could see him right away. The naval officer was as surprised as I was when I showed him the article. "Don't worry," he said, looking over his desk. "This is meaningless nonsense." He assured me there was no order to seize the *Feathered Serpent*. This was confirmed when he radioed Lima.

Down through the years I had had to contend with similar problems when complaints had been made through one branch of the government without the knowledge of the others. They could be most irritating.

I hurried down to the wharf. Two policemen informed me that the balsa was under quarantine. I was not allowed on board. Segundo, looking downcast, was standing on the dock. He had just put the finishing touches to the figureheads, which had dropped close to the waterline, so that their beards were actually touching the water. He had drawn the lines taut at the bowsprits. He said police inspectors had questioned him and then told him to get off the balsa so that they could inspect the cargo—which they were presently doing, going through everything with a fine-tooth comb. It was utterly ridiculous.

The best thing to do, it appeared, was to call Lima. I had to telephone *El Comercio* to give them a story anyway. Perhaps the editors of that very fine Peruvian daily could offer some suggestion. Returning to my hotel room, I was about to pick up the phone when there was a knock at the door. I opened it to discover two plainclothesmen. I asked for their credentials, which they showed me, and I let them in. Apologetically, they requested permission to inspect my luggage. After making a routine inspection of my belongings, they apologized again. I was now free to leave as soon as I cleared the local port authorities.

During the press interviews that followed, I explained the matter to the newsmen and invited them to the balsa to look for themselves. The next day we were fully exonerated. We never did discover who had made the accusation. Segundo thought the whole affair most amusing. Peruvians who have attained a certain status in the community are philosophical about such matters and consider it an honor to be haled into court. It is regarded as a sign of recognition. I never felt this way when it happened to me, but with the passing years I was able to recall with humor this story and many others like it.

I remember when our El Dorado expedition was brought to an abrupt halt. My men and I had uncovered the last of the seven Lost Cities of the Chachapoyas Kingdom and were in the process of making a fabulous new discovery when word arrived that a police patrol was hunting us down with orders to apprehend me on the proverbial treasure-robbing charge. Knowing that capture meant long confinement in the interior, I decided to make a run for it and make my escape over the Marañon River and thence to Lima. My Peruvian companions, knowing that the charges were trumped up by others to keep me from continuing my explorations, agreed to the challenge of helping me get away by muleback. I was led through secret mountain passages at altitudes of 13,000 feet above sea level, where we encountered blizzards, hail, and strong winds. They told me to pull a wool cap down over my head and crown it with an old straw hat. I was told to bury my face in my chest and not to look up under any circumstances. Wearing a poncho and disguised as a peasant, my muleteers explained to passers-by that I was ill with pneumonia and was being taken to the hospital. My guides thought this hilarious. In this way I was taken for just another unfortunate and was not questioned. The irony is that while I had spent four years exploring the area for archaeological remains, during the three days in which I made good my escape we passed through half a dozen old cities of which I was entirely ignorant and that had never been mapped. Even with the knowledge that a mounted police patrol was hot on our heels, it took all my willpower not to stop and record on film the vague images of magnificent stone masonry that I discerned from the corner of my eye.

Line drawing of the ruins of Gran Pajatén, Peru. Notable are the rectangular spiral and aquatic designs decorating the upper section of the circular building, which is approached by a stairway. The whole is built atop a series of terraced platforms resembling an artificial hill-pyramid. Drawing by Bill K. Dailey.

Crossing the Gulf of Guayaquil

Men at Sea

The *Feathered Serpent* left Port Talara at 0925 on April 28, 1969, her destination Manta, Ecuador. It was from this old port that the Peruvian Viracocha, accompanied by his disciples, made his exodus centuries ago and sailed away to Middle America where, I believed, he emerged as the Feathered Serpent.

A tug towed us out two miles. We cast off lines from the bouncing tug, hoisted the sail, and set a course of 330°, which would take us around Punta Lobos. Once we were well out to sea, we would alter course to due north across the Gulf of Guayaquil and head for Manta.

We had a scare the first half-hour or so. The balsa had been down by the head; now she was down by the stern, owing to Segundo's shifting our stores. She heeled to port, the stern float awash, the figurehead nearly touching the water. The strain on the sweep oar was tremendous. Big waves boiled over the stern and broke our tiller line. With a snap the line flew up in the air and the sweep oar struck my left side, throwing me to the deck with a crash. The oar swung over to port, shifting us to a course which would have run us aground in less than a half-hour. With the memory of the breakers at Talara fresh in our minds, we hurled ourselves on the sweep oar and put it hard to starboard. With the *Feathered Serpent* standing out to sea again, we lashed the sweep oar in place and slumped down on the deck totally exhausted.

Wind and Current Become the Masters

For an hour we held our course, then tacked north. The strong trade winds and the Peruvian current held us in their powerful system. A pod of dolphins sported about the balsa, and flying fish darted parallel to the *Feathered Serpent* as if racing her to Cabo Blanco. Every so often one would land with a thud on the bamboo deck and, before any of us could reach it, flip back into the water. As the day wore on, big seas rolled down upon us from the west, slamming into the side of the balsa with terrific force. Fearful of being pushed on the beach again during the night, we altered course and stood out to sea, watching the breakers pounding upon the shore. With the bows of the balsa pointing into the high waves, our speed was reduced to bare steerage, and when control of the balsa became marginal, we headed north again as the sun sank into the Pacific. After dark we could see the lights from Cabo Blanco fading away.

During the night a large tanker steamed across our bows to the south. We struggled at the helm, with the balsa riding over the crests of the waves and surfing down the other side into the deep troughs. The *Feathered Serpent* lurched, wrenched, and slammed through the hurtling seas. Drugged with sleep, we often came out on deck to assist the helmsman in his efforts to stay on course. This continued all through the night. With the coming of larger seas we were forced back to the original method of manhandling the oar from port to starboard helm with the force of our arms and backs. Whereas the balsa had steered herself for up to a half-hour at a time before, now we had to keep our eyes glued to the compass. If the course was allowed to change ten or fifteen degrees she would change from starboard tack to port, forcing the helmsman to untie the tiller lines, swing the oar over to the other side, and reset the sails. Oftentimes the balsa would alter course on her own before the helmsman could set the sails, and the whole operation would have to be repeated. Three or four such attempts and we were exhausted. Pride prevented us from calling for help, and we sat there, the balsa in irons, resting until we had strength enough to make another attempt.

Next morning, when the sun had burned through the patches of stratus clouds and I pointed my glasses to the west, there was no land in sight. We had left Cabo Blanco far behind and were now beating our way into the Gulf of Guayaquil. The balsa was still giving us great difficulty. There was no lashing the helm and hauling in the sheet as before. She simply would not sail close-hauled without further attention. We kept one hand on the tiller, another on the mainsheet, and both eyes on the compass. We shifted the stores forward and brought the stern float on the portside out of the water. But the *Feathered Serpent* persisted in her stubborn ways. Perhaps the barnacles, now becoming encrusted on the hull in ever increasing numbers, had changed the sailing characteristics of the balsa. They clung to the sweep oar in astronomical numbers.

At noon, the old port of Tumbez lay some eighty miles to the east of us. My mind went back to the days of the Inca king, Huayna Capac, when several of his captains and nobles were being transported on balsa rafts from the island of Puna to the coast. Once the Puna raftsmen were well out to sea, they untied the poles, and the Inca dignitaries fell into the water and drowned. Afterward the rafts were reassembled, and the raftsmen returned to the island and started a revolt. King

Huayna Capac put down the revolt with a fury that resulted in the death of thousands of the rebels.

The *Feathered Serpent* frothed along her northward course, drawing farther away from the shore. By midnight, when I went off watch, we were a hundred miles from the nearest land and away from the effects of the thirty-foot-high tides. Land would remain out of sight for nearly a week. Puna lay to the east at a point where the sun would come up next morning. On Wednesday morning, April 30, we continued to run with a following wind, and from the south came huge waves that hit the *Feathered Serpent* with periodic blows that sent shudders through her. If the violent pounding kept up, I was afraid she would not last. I had never experienced a strong gale from so close to the water (our feet were never more than six inches from the sea that swirled about the floats under the bamboo deck), and the sensation was terrifying. I estimated the wind to be force nine. The high waves that came streaking along were drawn up to a height of twenty-five feet or more by the forty-mile wind. But last she did, through most of the day, until the sea abated. I shall always remember her cutting through the seething waves. In late afternoon a miraculous transformation took place. Lazy clouds floated past in an electric blue sky, and the seas calmed. Schools of tuna ran parallel with us. Dolphins humped about, and giant sea turtles swam lazily by. Flying fish sped out of the water, became airborne and whizzed past, only to disappear into the sea again.

At sunset the next day, May 1, our seventeenth day out, the wind changed to light airs blowing in from the south and our sail hung slack. The longer we were out of sight of land, the more Segundo worried. With no way for us to make a land fix or sight a fishing boat, we might just as well have been floating in outer space, as far as he was concerned. I showed him our estimated position after calculating our daily run and told him I wanted to cut across the Gulf of Guayaquil in order to save time and avoid the fierce tides. This seemed to satisfy him. I relied on intuition and common sense in my navigation. Long exposure to the jungle had taught me that the physical senses were not reliable means of determining one's position in surroundings where visibility was limited to three or four feet. Of course the open sea was very different: Once we were out of sight of land, cross-currents could carry us west without our knowing it from a compass reading. Yet I knew that if we coursed north across the gulf, then steered east toward the rising sun, we would eventually make a landfall. I knew from which direction the seasonal winds blew, and if a contrary wind came up we could always heave to. Once the wind shifted we could hoist sail and continue east, much as the ancients must have done when sailing offshore between coastlines and out of sight of land. I had observed the wind's effect on the *Feathered Serpent* to be much greater than that of the current. My only fear was getting caught in a calm or doldrum where we could be at the mercy of westward-flowing currents.

Even the expert seafarers at Huanchaco were, like Segundo and the Peruvian natives in general, fearful of getting too far away from land. They took pains to keep their eyes on the sun's course through the sky. The Southern Cross points to the celestial pole, and even at night they could find a line on the south. It appeared clear to me that old Peruvian sailors would not have been prepared psychologically to give themselves up to the sea and drift helplessly west into the unknown. They would have used their experience to sail across the wind into the rising sun rather than surrender to the elements. It seemed to me that Pacific crossings in olden days would have been few and far between and their cultural significance almost negligible. Since we were now in westward-flowing currents, my theory would be put to the test in the days ahead.

Later in the day I logged:

> Flying fish keep popping on board during the night. Segundo gathers them in a basket each morning before they are washed overboard. They make a tasty meal when fried in canned Australian butter. Delicious as they are, I can never keep them down for more than a half-hour. My condition has become embarrassing. The coca tea and sea water stay down most of the time and give me strength.
>
> The antics of the flying fish are fascinating. They seem to be escaping from pursuing fish. Sometimes they land right in the mouth of larger fish, which catch them like football players taking in a pass. How the larger fish know where to wait is a mystery. Other times a big fish will jump out of the water and take a flying fish on the wing—after it has taken an aerial course of fifty yards.
>
> At noon, when I came off watch, I took out the radio and tuned to a Peruvian station. We listened to music throughout the rest of the day. Big rolling seas were coming in from the southeast. The *Feathered Serpent* was flung high, her sweep oar whipping back and forth like a reed in a windstorm. Oftentimes we hit the crest of a wave and surfed down into the trough. We were fearful that the steering oar would break and put us at the mercy of the sea.

The Giants of Santa Elena

At sunset I wrote in my log:

> The navigator gave our position as 25 miles off the coast of Santa Elena at 2° south latitude. He had us farther north again than my own calculations showed, and I

chose to continue our NNW in order to run with the wind. I am obsessed with getting as far north as possible, then cutting back to the coast when the winds change.

Thinking of Santa Elena took my memory back to something I had read in Pedro de Cieza de León's account of the Incas. The inhabitants of the area told a story, handed down from their remote ancestors, of giants who arrived in cane rafts from the sea and landed on their shores. The giants stood so tall, the locals hardly reached their knees. They were described as male, bearded, with long hair, and dressed in animal skins—or naked. They built a village on the spot and drilled through solid rock to reach fresh water. It is said they lived there for some time massacring the natives after having abused them. The story goes on to say that God sent an angel with a sword who killed them all for their practice of sodomy. Later their bodies were consumed by a heavenly fire, leaving nothing but bones. After the conquest certain Spaniards claim to have seen fragments of teeth that weighed half a pound. De León himself says that the natives should be believed because of the enormous bones noted in the area.

I had read Garcilaso de la Vega's recapitulation of this episode and the commentaries by later authors. Some have claimed a landing on the American coast from Polynesia, possibly from Easter Island. Others have speculated they were Vikings. While the former was possible, to my knowledge Vikings never used cane rafts. And what were they doing in the Pacific? It is more likely that the origin of these giants, if in fact they existed, was continental. As Bernardino de Sahagún recorded when writing about the ancient Toltecs of Mexico: "They were tall, larger in body than those who live today."

Inca Philosophers of the Sun

For the Incas the sun was more than a symbol of fertility, the life-giving source of earth's bounty. Like their contemporaries across the seas, the Incas saw a spiritual element as well. They worshiped Viracocha. In contrast, Aztec and Mayan priests of a perverted solar religion to the north believed that the sun gave life to the universe and that only by the blood sacrificed by man could it be nourished and given life. The Incas would have been horrified at the amount of blood shed by these peoples through wounds which they inflicted on themselves by driving maguey thorns into their tongues and cheeks; more so at the blood that spilled over the altars from human sacrifices. In this respect the Incas' teachings were closer to those of the Feathered Serpent, called by them Viracocha and known to the Mexicans as Quetzalcoatl and Kukulcan, who taught a mystic union between man and the cosmos through the medium of the sun. The idea of blood came at a later date, when ignorant priests dismissed the old teachings in order to get hold of the masses.

I watched the sun sink into the ocean, bathing cumulus clouds in pink. After it disappeared, darkness fell as suddenly as if someone had turned off a light in a room. A silvery moon rose up to replace the golden disk, casting rippling beams upon the quiet waters. As I sat in the stillness, listening to the waves splashing on the floats, my thoughts went back to the Inca kings who first contemplated the sun, and I spent the remaining hours at the bow speculating on the sun and its significance to ancient man. A few lines from Pharaoh Aknahton's "Hymn to the Sun" came to mind and I jotted them down in my log:

> Boats sail upstream and downstream . . .
> Before your face the fish leap out of the water,
> Your rays reach the green ocean.

It is you who places the male seed in women,
Who generates the semen in man.
You quicken the child in its mother's womb
And teach it not to cry.
Even in the womb you are the nurse.
You give breath to all creation,
And open the mouth of a newborn,
Giving it nourishment.
When the bird chirps from within the shell
You give it breath that it may live.
You bring its body into being,
So that it may break the egg.
And when it is hatched it runs
Announcing its creation into the world.

At the top of the page I had pasted a few lines from the *Desiderata* which had caught my eye years before. ". . . you are a child of the universe, no less than the tree and the stars; you have a right to be here. And whether or not it is clear to you, no doubt the universe is unfolding as it should. Therefore, be at peace with God, whatever you conceive Him to be . . ."

A Strange Experience

I slept fitfully. My whole body felt like a coiled spring; try as I might, I could not relax. My mind and spirit were a driving force within a body that was being pushed beyond the limits of its endurance. I had known for some time that I was demanding too much of it, living on a little tea and bits of food. It was as if I had been dealt a knockout blow, and while my instinct was to get up and fight, my legs and arms refused to obey the commands of my brain.

I lay trembling, in a cold sweat, faced with the horrible realization that my strength was running out of me like sand in an hourglass. The doctor in Lima had given me pills to relax, but I couldn't get them down. For an hour I tried to swallow a little water, but it was no use. The effort only made me throw up what little I had in my stomach, leaving me weaker than before. Then the gnawing pain, like a searing fire, worked at my insides. Finally I slept.

I awoke just before sunrise, with the spray from the bows hitting my face. I lay there awhile, listening to the waves rushing past and the wind in the rigging. The sounds soon put me to sleep again, and I was not aware of anything until the rays of the sun fell on my eyelids. I gazed curiously into the golden disk, until a kaleidoscope of colors and geometric designs swam before my vision. With the coming of the sun, the wind rose and the balsa took wing, rushing through the whitecaps toward a magnificent rainbow arched high in the sky, with both ends driving into the sea like giant iridescent pillars. It was as if I were mounted on a golden chariot racing toward the fiery sun through a sea of shimmering gold. Flying through the fine mist, spray-soaked, the *Feathered Serpent* twinkled and glowed like a comet. Suddenly the whole horizon was aglow with light. Like miniature suns my eyes were linked to the greater light now throbbing and oscillating from white to black and back to white again. A warmth and strength filled my whole being and I felt at one with all creation. The sea and the sky were no longer hostile. In that moment I loved everything; I experienced a feeling of benevolence, tolerance and understanding even toward those things I had hitherto feared. The swimming things in the sea were my brothers, as were the birds in the sky above. I felt as if I could communicate with lower forms of life, could make myself known and that they would respond in like manner.

As the light overflowed my being, much as wine might overflow a cup poured by an overgenerous host, something told me my consciousness was immortal, that I need not fear death or the adversities of this transitory world; that there was another world of permanence to which I was heir. For a split second I had no concept of time and my mind registered the wisdom of the universe. Like a computer it ticked off the mysteries of generations in a language of symbols that flowed from the sun like mathematical formulas through electric wires. I do not know how long I gazed into the sun; I was only vaguely conscious of Segundo shaking my shoulder, telling me it was my turn at the helm. I felt as light as a feather, as if I could walk on the sea, while making my way back to the deckhouse to attend to duties that now somehow seemed unreal and unimportant. I felt stronger. The sun had done it. I knew it inwardly.

May 2, 18th day out.

1200. The wind and current continue to carry us north across the gulf. The wind has dropped, but our speed is good. A dozen or more dorado fish, their aquamarine, blue, green, and golden colors glittering in the sun, continue to escort us. They circle the balsa day and night, swimming very close, as if it were a parent to which they were attached. Segundo is frustrated in his efforts to land one. He attaches a flying fish to the hook, hoping they will take it. When they do, they carry away the fish, hook, and valuable line. I have become so used to them I am glad when they break free. They are wonderful creatures that ignore the sharks which follow in our wake now that the dolphins have left us.

Life at sea has now become routine, and we are learning the idiosyncrasies of the balsa and how to keep her seaworthy and ourselves comfortable. Life is cramped, but a clean ship makes life easier. We bathe daily at the bows of the balsa, between the floats, away from the sharks. The fresh breeze and the sun feel good as we cover our bodies with coconut oil. This period of the day is one of our greatest joys. Segundo, as ship's carpenter—only one of his many duties—always manages to find something to repair. The navigator prefers rope, while the sail bags and the lines stowed at the bows have been left to me. Segundo and I are constantly hanging overside, tending to loose lines and making sure the bamboo framework is well secured to the floats.

Our diet is simple, and I am eating a little better. For the most part fish is the staple, supplemented with fresh and canned fruit. None of us really eat much, but we do drink liquids in generous amounts. The thermos bottles are kept filled with hot water so that each can pour the tea of his preference. While Segundo does the cooking, each man is responsible for his own wooden bowl and spoon. Dishwashing offers no problem, since we keep a keg of liquid sea soap on the portside of the deckhouse. It takes only a small amount of soap plus the foaming of the sea to keep a dish clean. We have found that the action of the sea water and the soap causes our clothing to deteriorate rapidly.

Segundo spends most of his idle time fishing. He takes care of his hooks, lines, lead weights, hand nets, and a large throwing net with weights, plus a gaff hook, as a surgeon would his instruments. He has become expert at fishing and there is always fish stew.

The navigator tinkers with the sextant, taking positions from time to time, and plots our course. My time is spent, when sea duties allow, recording the sounds of the expedition and filming in sequence whatever catches my eye. I try to shoot daily at least 200 feet of movie film and a 36-exposure roll of 35mm black-and-white film and an equal amount of color film. Keeping the cameras and lenses clean and dry is a task that in itself often keeps me up long after I have gone off watch at 2400. Tonight a blood-red moon rises up out of the sea to the east.

Surfing in Dangerous Seas

May 3.

1530. Strong wind and choppy seas late afternoon. The *Feathered Serpent* slithers along. Later we alter our easterly course and run north before the wind. The balsa rides up and over the crest of a wave, shooting forward with foam, then drops over and shoots down into the trough. Deep in the valleys we look up at the next wave approaching, afraid it will smash down upon us, sweeping the balsa out of control. But up rides the *Feathered Serpent* into another crest and over again like a roller coaster.

Once we lost control of her and she began to come about. We threw ourselves on the sweep oar, but our combined strength was not enough to put her back on course. The roar of the wind is terrifying and the sea heaves and moans, tossing us about like a paper boat in a whirlpool. The balsa slews completely around before rising to the top of the next crest. With the wind astern we struggle like crazed men to fill the sail and put her on course. Slowly the sail pops full and the bows begin to point her course again. We stand with mouths agape as we sweep down the wave, deep into the trough and up the other side, gripping the sweep oar, hanging on for dear life, afraid of being pounded to bits.

1600. I have been timing the big waves that roll in. On the hour and on the half-hour, tremendous waves thunder in from the open sea. The first one that hit scared the hell out of us. "Christ," Segundo yelled, staring open-eyed at the wave, "will you look at that!" But we bobbed over it like a wooden float.

1700. The float on the portside is much lower in the water. Waves cascade over the top of the float and splash the deck. The sail is trimmed and the sweep oar lashed to port helm as our course is now due east. Terrific seas batter the starboard float, and the balsa heels to portside. We begin shifting stores to starboard to compensate.

1730. Port float still low in water. For the first time we are afraid of totora becoming waterlogged. No matter. If floats submerge, upper deck will be out of the water and sail will propel us along. We seem to be carried north on the average of 30 miles daily and east about 24 miles. Anyway, we are moving closer to land. By day we point the bows to the rising sun and at night in the direction of the rising moon.

May 4, 20th day.

0900. I am much stronger today and feeling enthusiastic. Caught sight of a bright light to north on my watch last night. Probably lighthouse in Isla La Plata. Altered course due north and all hands kept alert through night. No sight of land.

0930. Segundo caught dorado this morning while bathing at bows. Curious fish swam up to investigate, and he took him with a gaff hook. It weighed about 20 pounds. It was beautiful when he brought it back to the working deck, but later turned a dirty gray.

1000. Many birds indicate land is near. All hands keep a sharp eye. Segundo runs up the Jacob's ladder to the crow's nest and surveys the horizon with his keen eyes.

1100. Sweep oar encrusted with myriads of barnacles. Floats thick with the little creatures that are slowing down our speed. Port float now awash at stern. Moved spare dagger-board to starboard.

1300. Sea calm. Light airs. More birds. No sign of land. We are not sure of our position. Lunched on tea, sea water, and a little milk with crackers. I simply cannot tolerate fish of any kind, fresh or canned. For the most part coca tea keeps me going, along with powdered milk and fruit. Sunrises seem to charge me with energy and I have no desire for food. Ribs hurting. Must have strained muscles while moving daggerboard.

1400. More birds. Bits of driftwood. Large sea turtle swims by. We are at mercy of current and prevailing wind which comes and goes, but ever steady from the south. I feel we will be carried to vicinity of Manta and have complete faith in my calculations. Viracocha and early seafarers who pioneered these sea routes must have been aided by the currents when trying to reach this port. Primitive navigation did not allow them to set a course as do powered vessels today. We have taken a chance by streaking across the gulf. Perhaps we should have made our way closer to the coast, but the near disaster at Talara has made us cautious.

1800. No sight of land. We are becalmed and drifting along with the current. Judging from chips of bamboo thrown into the water, our drift is slightly to the south and east. Are we being pushed into a bay?

On the morning of May 5, at 0930 hours, two fishing boats loomed over the northern horizon and were soon alongside. They identified themselves as the *Mariaelena* and the *Barracuda*, out of Manta. "Manta!" Segundo and I shouted in unison, grabbing each other and slapping each other's backs while jumping up and down on the deck like happy children. The navigator looked on incredulously. The fishermen seemed to share our enthusiasm and chatted back and forth, asking questions about our strange-looking vessel and disbelieving we were from Peru. They told us we were thirty miles due west of Manta and asked for some Peruvian coins. I found several twenty- and fifty-centavo pieces and handed them around, and Segundo threw them several cans of fruit juice. They sailed off and circled about, hauling in large tuna and bonito with hook and line. Later in the day a rowboat came over and two men bade us good day. Segundo shoved a message for the captain of the port into the hands of one of the fishermen and slapped him on the back, saying we would buy them drinks tomorrow. When they sailed off, Segundo jerked a thumb in the direction of the legendary port. "*Dios mío*," he said, "Manta, *por fin!*" With that we broke out the Ecuadorian and Peruvian ensigns, the Andean Explorers Club burgee, and the expedition pennants, dressing up the balsa in a rainbow of colors. Then we pointed our bows in the direction of the port.

Manta!

Next morning we awoke to discover land less than four miles dead ahead. A brilliant moon helped us during the night watches, though we saw no lights except those from a freighter that steamed past our port stern. We were not overly concerned about running aground, as the sea was calm. I was able to make out San Lorenzo to the south. Manta lay an estimated seven miles east of us. Several fishing skiffs with lateen sails circled about, and we were amazed at their rate of speed in the light airs, our own speed was very slow. I was saddened to see one hook a huge dorado fish from a line attached to the top of the mast that trails behind the wooden vessel. Three fishermen handled each boat in expert fashion. One of the speedy skiffs pulled up alongside, and the crewmen showed awe and wonderment when they examined the strangest vessel they had ever seen. They were thunderstruck to learn we hailed from Peru—probably no more than we were, to be so close to our destination. Then, just as suddenly as they came, they sailed away to attend to the day's fishing.

The wind fell and our sail flapped, giving us just enough steerage to make our way along the coast, now only a mile off the starboard beam. Although the sea was calm, dangerous currents swirled under the balsa, and we feared being pulled into the rocky shore. Just as a larger balsa of ancient times might have done, we hailed the smaller vessels, asking for a tow into the entrance of the bay. In a flash the skiffs pulled up alongside, took us in tow, and dropped us about half a mile north of the southern shore of the small peninsula. We waved good-bye, but not before Segundo had filled every hand with a can of our precious fruit, which he delighted in handing out, as if it had fallen from the sky.

We now found ourselves in a lane of busy diesel-powered tuna clippers making their way to and from Manta. It was unbearable to watch them move by, leaving us behind in their wake. When Segundo could stand it no more, I gave him permission to send a white flare arching into the gray sky to attract attention. We did not have the patience of the ancients; nor did we want to run the risk of a collision that night with one of the many vessels in the busy harbor, a danger which former seafarers did not have to face.

We were taken in tow by the first clipper heading for port, and I ran up a yellow flag requesting permission to enter port.

At 1330 hours on the afternoon of May 6, twenty-two days after departing from Salaverry, we entered Manta, old Port of Viracocha, 0° 57′ south latitude. A customs launch came out and piloted us to a berth in front of the port authority. I was amazed at the hundreds of people standing on the jetty to welcome us. On stepping ashore we were greeted by Captain Gabriel Garrido-Zambrano, who showed us every courtesy through customs.

After brief ceremonies and a short press conference, we made our way through the throng on wobbly legs, the land swimming before our eyes.

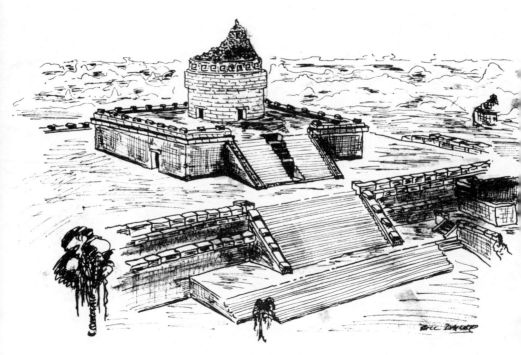

Sketch of the observatory or caracole at the Mexican ruins of Chichén Itzá. This circular building is built atop a rectangular base and approached by stairways similar to those of Gran Pajatén. Note the rectangular spiral fretwork. Drawing by Bill K. Dailey.

—◆—

Manta, Port of Viracocha

The Feathered Serpent *Crashes into the Sea*

The city of Manta had boasted a population of 20,000 souls when the first Spanish ships made port here as early as 1527. The harbor was lined with sailing balsawood rafts that carried up to thirty tons of cargo. Bartolomé Ruiz de Estrada encountered one of these off the coast, transporting pieces of gold and silver—crowns, diadems, belts, armor—and rich clothing, emeralds, pearls, and conch shells. But the Spaniards had other fish to fry. Francisco Pizarro, led by pilot Ruiz, went on to conquer Peru.

In 1534, Pedro de Alvarado, governor of Guatemala, arrived in Manta with a fleet of eleven ships. Four hundred troops were set ashore looking for the temple treasure, rumored to consist of gold, pearls, and a giant emerald the size of an ostrich egg. When this booty escaped the Spaniards, the city was looted and burned and a large number of prisoners taken as slaves. Eight years later the city was sacked by pirates. By the year 1605 the native population was barely 1,600. In 1607 and again in 1608 Manta was destroyed by pirates. The 1921 census of Ecuador showed the city with a population of 4,000—a big drop from its former glory.

Today the city is a modern tropical port with marine facilities that include a large crane. Ships of all nationalities come and go. I was glad to see that the modern city had not buried its past. The primitive fishing skiffs with their patchwork sails dart in and out of the harbor, lending color to the background of gleaming white buildings and blue water. The fishermen, young and old, gather around the docks in the early afternoon to weigh and sell their catch. Legends drift into conversations. They speak of the one-eyed giants who lived amongst them centuries earlier, and of Tupac Yupanqui's balsa voyage to the mysterious islands beyond. They tell of the nymphs who blow on conch shells, and of the goddess of the sea who never fails to receive part of the catch to assure health and good fortune. One name never fails to appear: Viracocha, the fair-skinned superhuman lord who arrived from the south with bearded disciples, teaching moral codes and peace, healing the sick, and making the blind to see. After a time he sailed away, promising to return.

After resting, I went to the telegraph office and sent off several telegrams to New York and Lima. Shortly thereafter teletypes began clacking out the news of our safe arrival.

MANTA, MAY 6, ECUADOR—AT 1330 TODAY THE BALSA KU-VI-QU PUT IN THIS EASTERN PORT IN CENTRAL ECUADOR AFTER MAKING A VOYAGE OF 250 MILES SINCE LEAVING TALARA LAST TUESDAY. SAVOY DECLARED THE EXPEDITION IS USING OLD SEA ROUTES AND WILL VISIT VARIOUS PORTS AS WAS DONE BY ANCIENT AMERICANS WHEN SAILING ALONG THE CONTINENTAL COASTLINE.

From *El Comercio, Lima, Peru*

The news told only part of the story. A great deal was to be done. I drove down to the port authority and complimented the captain on the marina, telling him it was the best I had seen. I explained how important it was to pull the balsa out of the water and make repairs on the centerboard, if possible, and remove the barnacles. This would allow us to give the undersides a general inspection and dry out the totora, as was done by the ancients. Making a study of the totora floats, line, and knots was nearly as important as making the voyage itself. I had considered rolling her up on the beach, for which she was designed, but he advised against it. He suggested instead that we take her out of the water with one of the cranes and put her on the dock behind locked gates with guards round the clock. There we could make all the observations we wanted, with full assurance that she would be safe from the curious spectators who were already milling about the docks by the thousands. In this way spectators could be admitted at regular hours. With this I agreed.

Next morning, the *Feathered Serpent* was moved from her berth in front of the captain of the port's office and towed by powerboat to the end of the breakwater at the marine terminal. All this was taking place while I was showering. When I arrived at the pier, Segundo was in the water with several native swimmers, placing large wooden beams under the floats. One-inch polyethylene rope had been secured to these and attached to a marine crane. I figured that the test strength for this line was about six tons. Waterlogged as she was, the balsa's weight couldn't have been less than six tons and was probably closer to seven. This was cutting it pretty thin. I dashed over to the navigator and told him to hold everything, but he waved me off, saying, "The rope is strong. Don't worry. It can take twice the load." With this he motioned for the crane operator to go ahead.

I realized that the stevedores were sincere and that their time was at a premium. Only one hour had been allotted and they wanted to get on with it. However, the entire expedition was at stake. I had visions of the balsa dropping into the water with a crash. I scurried through the milling crowd toward the crane operator; he stopped the motor, stuck his head out of the cabin, and asked me what I wanted.

"Is there any five-inch hawser around?" I asked. He shook his head. Six or seven stevedores came over. I explained I wanted heavier rope. They shrugged. Someone went looking for one but returned a few minutes later empty-handed. By this time the navigator had shuffled over with the foreman. I was assured the line was sufficient and was told not to worry; he accepted full responsibility. The foreman took his side and put a friendly hand on my shoulder. I told him to go ahead, cautioning the crane operator to take it slow and easy and let the water drain off when she came out of the water. He agreed and everyone returned to work.

Making my way through the throng, pressed to the very edge of the wharf, I looked down at the *Feathered Serpent* rocking gently to and fro on the soft swells thirty feet below. I heard the crane operator start the engine and watched as the lines tightened. The balsa quivered, then rose out of the water. Then, with a loud crack, one of the beams broke. The balsa settled back into the water. Another beam was lowered by rope, and Segundo had it put in place under the floats at the stern, except that this time the ropes were moved in closer to the center to put less strain on the heavy eight-inch beams. I insisted the lines be slung underneath the balsa as a safety measure. The operation was begun a second time.

True to his word, the crane operator lifted the balsa gently, holding it steady when it was two feet above the surface of the harbor. Rivulets of water gushed out of the cane and totora like a waterfall. When it had drained sufficiently, the operator began lifting it by degrees. The lines grew taut under the weight as the great barnacle-encrusted hulk rose slowly upward, like a wounded walrus on a hook. I could see that the weight was too much. Up it came . . . three, four, five, six feet above the water. The lines hummed with energy, and I thought I heard a moan, as if the *Feathered Serpent* knew what was about to happen. I called to the crane operator to stop, but he didn't hear me because of the noisy crowd. She came up, ten, twelve, fifteen feet. I held my breath, my heart in my throat. Then it happened. The stern lines snapped with a loud twang and I envisioned her plummeting stern first into the sea, breaking apart like so much kindling. Quick as a flash the crane operator let go the lines, and the *Feathered Serpent* dive-bombed straight down on an even keel. In that terrible moment I saw the expedition done for. I stood petrified. The crowd gave out a great shout.

It took what seemed an eternity for her to cover the fifteen feet. She hit with a terrific force, sending up a great geyser of spray and foam. By some miracle she hit flat. With a sickening thud all four prows pancaked, striking the water like a dead swan, her back broken by the impact. The spars teetered and fell forward, sending the Andean Explorers Club burgee fluttering to the deck.

On our way to the docks the next morning the whole affair seemed like a nightmare, unreal and ridiculous.

When we passed through the gates, the guards were pleasant enough, but brief. The stevedores, usually friendly, avoided conversation. They had seen the balsa, or what was left of it, and, as if understanding our plight, left us alone. It was embarrassing being indulged in this way. Seeing a broken ship is a sad event among seamen, and I knew their sympathy was deeply felt.

The balsa, broken and lifeless, lay inert. A ghostly calm enveloped her. Only the soft whine of the wind through her slack rigging, and the gentle swells of the tide splashing the piers, made any sound. For the better part of the morning Segundo and I examined the balsa carefully. After twenty-three days in the water the totora was swollen but in good condition. The barnacles covering the undersides could be scraped off when she dried. She had taken a great deal of punishment when she hit the water. The superstructure was definitely out of kilter. Lopsided is a better word, for the starboard float was much lower than the port float. This was perhaps the worst damage sustained by the *Feathered Serpent,* and it would alter her sailing characteristics considerably. The general damage report, taken from the log, read as follows:

1. Superstructure out of alignment. Several bamboo canes broken. Must be replaced.
2. Working platform out of kilter. Starboard higher than port. Many canes splintered. Must be replaced.
3. Mast step damaged. Must be replaced.
4. A-frame sprung. Must be straightened.
5. Under-fender in fair condition. Some canes to be replaced.
6. Centerboard or *guare* splintered. Lodged between bundles and cannot be pulled out and replaced.
7. All four prows damaged beyond repair. Must be replaced.
8. Figureheads broken. Must be replaced.
9. Our 40-foot spar for large sail broken. Must be replaced.
10. All lines must be tightened.
11. Deckhouse looks like Leaning Tower of Pisa. Don't know what can be done.
12. Sextant and cameras will have to be checked. No damage noted.
13. Chronometer must be calibrated from shock of fall. Also compasses.
14. Damage to assorted gear such as lamps, stove, etc. Must be replaced.

Even with a broken back the balsa would float, thanks to the Huanchaqueros who had built a strong vessel. We made a list of materials needed for the repairs, and Segundo said he could have her ready in a week if given a local shipwright as helper.

Not only was he ship's carpenter, but more than anyone else he had firsthand working knowledge of the vessel. Here on the coast of Ecuador, no shipwright had ever seen, much less constructed, a balsa made of reeds. Segundo delighted in his authoritative position. The navigator, somewhat subdued, kept out of his way except to offer his help. Segundo never mentioned wanting to go home again.

By noon, plans to repair the *Feathered Serpent* had moved from theory to fact. Augustín Jiménez, manager of the marine terminal, gave us permission to make repairs on the dock and provided us with guards. A shipwright was employed. Good *caña de Guayaquil* was available in abundance, so repairs could begin immediately. Fortunately I had taken the precaution of ordering several *cargas* of totora and four extra serpent-figureheads in advance, for just such an emergency. In addition to making repairs, I decided to convert the *Feathered Serpent* into a genuine drift-type watercraft of the most primitive shape and design. Weakened as she was by the crash, we couldn't hope to restore the balsa to her former self without taking her completely apart and rebuilding her from the bottom up. That was beyond our skill and resources here in Manta. With all the strained and broken lines, she would probably fall apart right under our feet in the first heavy sea. To remedy this we decided to lash the totora bundles together with heavy line. In addition, I instructed Segundo to add bamboo double-pontoon floats at the sides and lash them to either totora float. The end result would be a bulky cargo-type raft of the most cumbersome design incorporating primitive ideas.

Rebuilding the Balsa

The following day the metamorphosis of the *Feathered Serpent* began. The navigator went off somewhere to have the sextant and chronometer calibrated. He returned in the afternoon to declare "an eighteen-minute error in the sextant and the chronometer running six minutes behind." When Segundo heard this he laughed up his sleeve, winked one of his lustrous black eyes at me, and shook his head. "Who's he trying to fool?"

Wanting to visit the local museum and study the archives, I left Segundo and the shipwright to carry on repairs. When I left they were working on a new rudder-oar design. Four helpers were doing the routine work. Next day Tom Spain and Dan Aldrich of CBS filmed the reconstruction and taped interviews. With that out of the way, I drove out to Puerto Viejo to talk to the local people and to gather notes on the legends and folklore of the region. They were spellbound to learn that we were on the trail of the Feathered Serpent. Most agreed that he had gone on to Mexico when leaving Ecuador. It was interesting to note that their mythology included stories of whole communities living on floating balsas, much the same as do the Uru Indians today on Lake Titicaca in Peru.

On the morning of May 11 (Sunday), after five days in port, I went down to the dock to find that the modifications were progressing well. Two bundles or pontoon floats, each consisting of fourteen bamboo canes five inches thick and about twenty feet long, were lashed to the sides. These were unsightly. A new rudder oar was attached, the figureheads had been replaced, the A-frame mast was straightened, and new rigging had been put in. When the backstays and forestays were tightened, the balsa began to resemble a sailing vessel once again. The deckhouse was still lopsided, but there was nothing we could do about that. Additions were made to the centerboards by plugging the originals with wooden pegs. I wasn't too keen on this idea because I didn't think they would hold.

Four hundred and fifty liters of canned water and food for sixty days were stored in a nearby warehouse until the *Feathered Serpent* was put into the water. Weight was no problem as it had been in Salaverry. With the addition of the bamboo floats we could have carried several tons of cargo without affecting the balsa unfavorably.

I put the radio ashore, choosing to go back to primitive navigational methods. Without the aid of radio communication or organized navigation we would be duplicating the conditions of the old days. I did retain the distress transmitter for emergency, however. I was convinced, as was Segundo, that navigational instruments in the hands of our navigator were of little practical value. Indeed, they were more of a hindrance. We decided to put our faith in the currents, the wind, and our own observations of sun, stars, and land. The navigator never learned of our decision.

On May 12 there was some trouble at the docks. I had dropped in to inspect the work and found the navigator behind some loading platforms cutting up an American flag I had received from a ship's officer the day before. I was utterly speechless. He was using a large pair of scissors, and three full-length stripes and a dozen stars lay on the dock at his feet. When he saw me his face flushed. "It's too large," he said. "I am making it smaller like the others." Boiling mad, I grabbed it out of his hands and picked up the remnants. I took the pieces into the deckhouse and placed them in a plastic bag and stowed them away in my locker. Then I ran up the smaller flag.

Segundo was grumpy and in a bad temper. I supposed he dreaded the idea of going back to sea. I was a little irritable myself, so I knew how he felt. He had been working hard. He came into the deckhouse and sat on the bunk. "Gene," he said, "from now on we sail as friends. I take orders from no one.

I'll do my job, have no fears. When we return to Lima I'm going home, back to the jungle where I belong. Will you accept me on these conditions?"

I studied him for a moment and slapped him on the back. "Fine, Segundo. We are three men on a raft." I pushed a hundred-sucre note into the palm of his hand and told him to take the afternoon off. He brightened and went back to work.

Shortly after this, the navigator sauntered in and insisted on being the skipper. He said he would take me anywhere I wanted to go. "You are the director of the expedition, but I am the captain." His haughtiness was so unbelievable I hardly knew what to say. I had never encountered anyone quite like him. I considered sending him back to Lima on the next plane; but the hurricane season would sweep Central America beginning in June or July, and there was little time to look for another hand. God help us if we ever got caught in one of those 125-mile-an-hour blows. "All right," I replied casually, "you be the captain and I'll be the admiral. How's that?"

My words seemed to satisfy him and he started to leave; then, turning around, he said, "Even the admiral sits at the right side of the captain of the ship when dining." With that he left. It was utterly fantastic. It happened on all my expeditions sooner or later. Almost everyone, from the chief porter to the head muleskinner, wanted to be the leader in one way or another. I had had problems with Segundo on this account before. I never deprived any man of the right to do his own job, or to make an impression on the others. It was an old story. When men work together, the aggressive instincts come out. Our small working deck was to be our whole world for weeks on end, and here we were, fighting for territorial rights as if we were apes in the primordial jungle. Had we not been living so close to the sea, or had the conditions been less hostile, it might have been different. I couldn't help thinking at the time that higher values are possible only when the necessities of life are met and the rigors of nature overcome. I found myself appreciating civilization much more than ever before, not only for the comforts it extends, but for the higher ideals that are possible within it. Only when material needs no longer dominate one's being can the individual push his own ego into the background and work for a common good.

On Tuesday, May 13, the balsa was lowered into the water by means of the crane in the marina and a five-inch hawser that someone had dug up. Earlier in the day it had rained, and when the sun came out, it was hot and sticky. Ordinarily we would have sailed under these conditions, but I wasn't taking any chances. Unlucky or no, the thirteenth wasn't a day for embarking on a dangerous coastal run in a makeshift balsa raft. In this respect I was a superstitious sailor. We put the stores aboard and moored the balsa in front of the port authority. Leaving a guard on watch, we took the day off, our last day in the hospitable city of Manta where we had been treated like long-absent brothers.

*Mexican ruins of Labna, Yucatán, showing zigzag motif similar to
the Peruvian Gran Pajatén ruins. Sketch by Bill K. Dailey.*

———◆▶——

Stranded on a Shoal

First of the Sea Serpents

At 0900, with all flags flying, the *Feathered Serpent* was towed out of the harbor by the *Don Ramona*, a forty-five-foot diesel-powered fishing boat. We arced three signal rockets into the blue sky as a farewell salute to the crowds lining the dock and breakwater. Hardly anyone noticed that the additions to our centerboards popped to the surface and floated away in our wake. Two miles out, an Ecuadorian gunboat, *Corvette LC 72*, steamed by, her decks lined with dignitaries waving good-bye. Captain Garrido's voice came over the bullhorn wishing us godspeed. We dropped our towlines and hoisted the sail. The gunboat stood off, circled, then steamed over the horizon. Light three-knot airs from the south pushed us along the shoreline, the sea heaving with gentle swells and the sky completely cloudless.

Next day several snakes swam by, and Segundo tried to reach one with a pole. He poked at its yellow-and-black body flattened from side to side for easier swimming, but it filled its lungs with air and disappeared under the water. He showed surprise when I told him it was a sea snake—*Pelamyrus platurus* —related to the coral snake—whose bite would result in death in three to four hours. The navigator laughed and said it was nothing but a harmless eel. I suggested that Segundo haul one aboard and examine its mouth for himself; he knew enough about jungle snakes to tell whether it was a poisonous reptile or not. He propped a pole against the deckhouse in readiness. Looking for a specimen became his principal project for days to come.

In the early afternoon a fishing boat with patched sails came alongside and sent over a canoe with a gift of fish. Before I could stop him, Segundo gave them two gallons of cooking oil in an expensive plastic container. Right after this a gentle breeze began to blow at ten knots. Our speed was considerably slowed down by the cane bundles, but we clipped along at a steady pace. Around midnight we rounded Cabo Pasado.

On May 16, the thirty-second day of the expedition and the third day out of Manta, I entered the following in my log:

1100. Hope to cross the equator sometime today. Old sailors say you feel the bump when you cross. Nothing like this so far. At 0600 light airs with wind from SE averaging 2 mph. At 0800 this increased to light breeze of 6 mph from SW. At 1000 we were becalmed. We put up the Dacron sail in hopes of catching at least a wisp of wind. I wish we had light cotton sails like those used by the fishermen at Manta; the canvas is too heavy. Shortly after the calm set in, a CBS News plane found us and made several passes over the *Feathered Serpent*. It circled around for 45 minutes, then disappeared to the south. It would be our last communication with them for many weeks. We are 8 miles offshore. Have logged 50 miles in last 48 hours. Current propels us about 8 miles per day. Thank goodness for trade winds, light as they may be. Currents will increase in force farther north. Everyone is in excellent spirits now that we are at sea. I told Segundo, in a conciliatory way, not to give

away any more food, especially oil and canned fruit.
The men need oil for frying fish, and I have discovered
that oatmeal and fruit make a wonderful meal that stays
down. He agreed but admonished me to start eating what
the sea produces, as did the ancients; only in this way
could I expect to get along with the sea and become one
with it. "People of the jungle follow the same rule,"
he said.

The balsa lay becalmed, the air hot and clammy, leaving us
all steaming with sweat. The light from the sea was intense
and made us screw up our eyes. We went around barefooted,
stripped to our shorts. The deckhouse was unbearable and I
wrote my notes at the prows, afraid to put my feet into the
water for fear of being bitten by sea snakes or sharks. As the
day wore on I directed my thoughts to another world, and how
I longed for the cool air of the uplands of Peru. At 1400 hours
a light breeze returned from the south and continued through
the night. Several fishing boats, attracted by our running lights
and the big white light reflected on our sail, came by for short
chats during the night.

Light airs and calms continued through the seventeenth. We
were averaging approximately eight hours of wind out of each
twenty-four, and even those were fairly light. The wind began
to blow around noon and strengthened to nine to ten knots by
midafternoon. Keeping our stern pointed to the south became a
real challenge on both day and night watches. Those on free
watch had to assist the helmsman, for he was not able to do it
alone. Even with light airs we wanted to take advantage of
every forward motion. By currents alone the journey would
take four months to Panama, twice that to Mexico.

The odor of drying anchovies hung over the *Feathered
Serpent*. Segundo, with the hand net, had made his daily catch

of the tiny silvery fish, cleaned them, and placed them on wooden boards to dry in the sun. He hooked two large dorados and an assortment of other fish, which he cleaned and dressed out for the pan.

Crossing the Line

According to my estimates, we crossed the equator at longitude 80° 45′W around 0100 Sunday, May 18, the thirty-fourth day of the voyage. Leaving the Southern Hemisphere was a conquest in itself. Right after breakfast the navigator, dressed up in a long wool poncho, handmade whiskers, and long flowing hair made from hemp and carrying a gaff hook as a trident, emerged out of the deckhouse as Father Neptune to christen Segundo, the only one who had never crossed the line.

"Who dares enter my kingdom?" said Neptune.

"I, Segundo."

"Why have you come?"

"To obtain your blessings."

"Very well, kneel."

Segundo, sweating in the hot afternoon sun and wearing only a pair of shorts, dropped to his knees. From a large gourd Father Nep poured sea water over his head, touching him on the shoulder with his trident. "I christen you," he said. "Arise, my son." With that he disappeared to the bow, leaving Segundo and me dissolved in laughter.

A few minutes after the ceremony, Segundo landed a six-foot shark that had been trailing in our wake for hours. He had baited a large hook attached to a piece of chain on a heavy nylon cord with a fat anchovy, and the shark took it. Segundo clubbed it lifeless with a wooden stick and hauled it aboard with a gaff hook. I think he hated sharks as much as snakes.

We were running parallel to the shoreline at a distance that averaged ten to fifteen miles. A steady eight-to-ten-knot wind came in from the southwest. The coastal branch of the Peruvian current that flows into Panama Bay impelled us ever northward, but at a slower speed than it had farther south. Sometimes the wind dropped off altogether, and the risk of being becalmed and set ashore by a countercurrent kept us a respectable distance from land. We were in the shipping lanes and had been catching sight of freighters, tankers, and tuna clippers daily. We must have made an odd sight indeed, what with our colorful sail and figureheads mounted on a golden ship of bamboo and straw. When the stars came out, the Southern Cross with its four points was low in the horizon, and I could not make out the Pole Star, though theoretically it should be visible from the equator. I estimated that our daily run was thirty-five miles or so. Just before going off watch I recorded:

2300. Many sharks circling balsa. Can see them with flashlight. There is a cricket on board. Must have made its home in the bamboo cane at Manta. Its chirping is most pleasant. Many insects attracted to our lights. Spotted a streaking object in the sky which proved to be a satellite.

With daybreak on the nineteenth the wind fell light, and we ghosted along in sight of land. A score of sharks circled the balsa and milled about between the stern floats near the rudder oar. We rigged up some lifelines just in case someone lost his footing. Segundo had been watching them for several days, frustrated because they interfered with his fishing. He grabbed the big butcher knife that lay on the cutting board and lashed it to a long bamboo pole with some nylon cord. Then he waited, and when one of the creatures got close enough, he drove the twelve-inch blade into its side all the way up to the hilt. The injured ten-footer thrashed madly about, rolling over and over, throwing up a maddened sea of foam and blood. There was an explosion of gray forms as a dozen or more sharks zoomed into the picture to investigate the death convulsions of their comrade. Frenzied by what he saw, Segundo hit several more of the sinuous forms. When the knife worked loose from the pole he took it in hand, climbed out on the bowsprit and hacked away at the shapes. Afraid he would be injured, I called out, but he paid no attention at all. This was to be his favorite sport in the weeks ahead. After this incident I wrote in my log: "Hope to get in the currents a little to the north that can carry us 12 to 30 miles each 24 hours. Light airs, less than 1 mph, are getting us nowhere fast. Late afternoon, jungled cliffs of Cabo Tortuga came into view. Wonderful to see green forests from the outside."

We had been throwing coconut shells, banana peels and bits of bamboo into the water to estimate our progress. But with land in sight we could judge better. At 1800 hours we rounded Punta Galera, noting our true run over the preceding twenty-four-hour period to be forty miles.

On May 20 I wrote:

> Still raining. Dolphin escort has chased away the sharks, much to our relief. One of our fears is falling overboard during the night watch with nobody to help. Dolphins snorted about for the better part of two hours, then swam off. Sharks did not return.

On May 21 Cabo Manglares appeared off the starboard bow at first light. Wind and current had pushed us some ninety miles since rounding Cabo Galera thirty-six hours before. The *Feathered Serpent* skitted right into Colombian waters sometime during the early morning. We hauled down the Ecuadorian flag and hoisted the Colombian ensign on the starboard rigging. The temperature dropped to 84° F. and I pulled on a sweater in the gentle breeze from the southwest.

Our waterline, lengthened by the conversion at Manta, had been extended to thirty feet, and the totora reed floats were low in the water at the bow and stern so that the Turk's-head whiskers of the figureheads dragged in the water. We were no longer concerned that the balsa might become waterlogged, as the cane float additions kept us high and dry. Our freeboard was one foot above the sea. During watch one could look down between the deck bamboos and observe the anchovies swimming between the floats, off in the shadows out of the sun. Like a magnet the *Feathered Serpent* had drawn to herself an entire entourage of living things. There were hundreds of fish of every size and variety. The dorado fish were always there, circling our floating island and tagging behind like chicks following a mother hen. One day the sharks would dominate the scene, only to be chased off by the dolphins, which would sport around us for days on end. Our little family included three flies that buzzed about in orbit, a single moth, two little white spiders and, of course, the cricket. I had counted a dozen or more other insects—six ants, two earwigs, four caterpillars—and couldn't help wondering if they were aware of their precarious abode. When we ran close to shore, clusters of driftwood floated by, their undersides teeming with copepods the size of your fingernail. We used to fish out pieces of wood worn into interesting forms by the sea until we discovered a sea snake coiled around a floating board. From then on driftwood was strictly taboo. Myriads of butterflies joined the menagerie and fluttered about our heads. Masses of Portuguese men-of-war floated past, their translucent mauve-and-pink forms brilliant in the sunshine. Once a Galápagos turtle, sunbathing in the current, flapped by as if it didn't have a care in the world—that is until Segundo said the word "soup" and reached for a gaff hook.

It raised its head when it saw (or heard) us and swam off.

The following night we ran into a storm. The rain came down in sheets through all watches. The sea heaved like moving mountains and valleys, and the foam-laden wind blew in from the southwest with a roar. We trimmed the sail and fought to keep from being swept overboard. Up went the safety lines, and we put on our lifebelts. No one man could handle the helm alone, and it was all the three of us could do to keep her on course. Conserving our energy, we moved about the deck slowly and efficiently. When the weather subsided hours later, we were glad to crawl into a dry and comfortable deckhouse and sleep the sleep of the dead.

Come morning, the navigator bellowed from the stern to come out on deck. Segundo and I, fearing the worst, stumbled over each other getting out of the deckhouse. Outside we found the helmsman holding up a sixty-pound sea turtle that he had taken with a gaff hook moments before. He was a beautiful creature, intelligent-looking, with an air of benevolence about him. He offered no protest at all when the men sported with him, and would have crawled back into the sea if someone hadn't rolled him over on his back. I was for returning him to the sea—after all, he hadn't harmed us and we didn't need the food. But the navigator wanted the shell as a souvenir and Segundo had in mind filet of turtle soup.

We had rigged an extra piece of canvas on the roof of the deckhouse and collected twenty gallons of fresh water during the storm. With fresh water falling from the sky and plenty of fish and turtle meat at our fingertips, we were living off the sea.

For some unknown reason we kept dropping our knives, forks, and spoons overboard. Once they hit the split bamboo deck there was no recovering them; they would disappear into the sea before we could put a hand on them. I spent the entire day of May 22 whittling a spoon out of a piece of wood I had found lodged between the bamboos and the deckhouse near the rain barrels portside earlier in the day.

On Friday, May 23, an incredible blood-red-orange morning began a golden day. Meeting the sun had become a ritual. Its life-giving rays warmed my body and cheered my soul; often, weather permitting, I slept on the foredeck under the sail so as not to miss it. I attributed my improving health to it. My appetite had returned, and swallowing became a little easier. Sometimes I would chew a handful of coca leaves to relax my throat muscles, then drink a cup of coca tea. I made a resolution to force myself to eat, no matter how great the effort. The best aid was to relax and stop worrying. I discovered that by slowing down and withdrawing into myself I could actually control the esophagus and open it up far enough to get down a bowl of oatmeal mixed with canned fruit and pulverized minerals and vitamins. I would feel the food traveling down and jamming up in the restricted passage. After much concentration, or whatever it was I was learning to do, the passage would loosen like a spring unwinding, and the food would drop of its own accord. This experience taught me that involuntary body functions can come under the voluntary control of the brain and nervous system once a technique is mastered. In spite of this partial control I had an insatiable craving for water and for being able to gulp it down in one long swig. This I couldn't do. I used to sip a cup of sea water two or three times a day which, while not satisfying, did replace the salt lost through perspiration.

Becalmed and ghosting along on a glassy sea, we took advantage of our first day off since leaving Manta. Before going on watch I made an inspection of the floats. The gooseneck barnacles had not returned, and everything, including the totora, bamboo, and lines, was in top shape. I coiled the lines at the foredeck and checked the safety lines of the sail bags, gave the life preservers, safety lines, and dinghy the once-over, and climbed up the Jacob's ladder to the crow's nest and examined the crosstree, rigging, and masthead. With that out of the way I swept the horizon with my binoculars—no sight of land—then took over the helm.

Sitting alone in the quiet (the navigator had turned in for a snooze and Segundo was at the bows making his daily ablutions), I leaned my back up against the deckhouse and stretched out my legs to relax. As I peered from under my cap at an evaporating sea that boiled under a rising tropical sun, my imagination placed a string of old sailing balsas off the port quarter. I could almost hear the shouts of men, the trumpeting conch shell blown by an authoritative witch doctor calling for wind; see the smoke curling up from charcoal fire on the fantails; and smell roasting fish and herbs rolled up in banana leaves. What they said and thought has not survived. To know and understand what the ancients thought, one has to relive their experiences. Sailing on a primitive vessel such as the *Feathered Serpent* brought the past into sharper focus. The expedition had proved to be one thing in principle, quite another in practice. Cut off from land and the ways I had known there, faced with the fury of the elements as were men a thousand years or more ago, I learned the meaning of what it was like to go to sea. My senses were sharpened and I grew to appreciate even the most simple needs—a good night's sleep, a common meal, and a peaceful day. Civilized men often take for granted the benefits of society and complain when life doesn't give them what they think is coming to them. Life doesn't give us anything. We are aliens living in a hostile world, and it is only by our own work and ingenuity that we are able to survive. The sooner men recognize this fact, the sooner they will understand the beautiful thoughts of the ancient wise man who emphasized the need of living and working with nature.

At 2400 I went to the foredeck with my sleeping bag under my arm. I curled up with my head on a coil of rope, taking in the stars and a glorious moon. It had been a wonderful day for all of us and I felt refreshed. The balsa was surrounded by an escort of dorado fish aglow in the moonlight. I counted some three hundred radiant fish. The flapping sail woke me twice during the night. I didn't mind—it meant we were moving with the wind.

On May 24, the fortieth day of the voyage, we logged close to fifty-five miles. Wind and currents had carried us approximately twenty-five miles northeast of the island of Gorgona. From the abundance of sea birds about the balsa, the type of fish, the smell of forests, the insects in the air, and the offshore wind that started to blow every night, like clockwork, around 2300 hours I could tell that we were approximately twenty miles offshore. This was pretty primitive navigation, if indeed it could be called that, but that's what the expedition was all about. Wind and current were doing the piloting.

An enormous school of sharks swarmed around the balsa most of the day. They appeared highly agitated, as if something were chasing them. I had never seen them in such numbers before—or so large. Two or three measured fifteen feet long. They smacked up against the sides of the floats. We were afraid they might damage the rudder oar. One big fellow raced under the balsa and struck the starboard cane fender with such impact that the *Feathered Serpent* shuddered. Infuriated, Segundo slithered out on the sternsprit starboard and started hacking away at the milling sharks with the butcher knife. He hit one, then another, with blows that seemed to be meant for the whole world. I hated to see him risk his life in such a manner, but there was no stopping him. Once he had fought a puma bare-handed and killed it by driving his fist down its throat. With a fury he struck one after another of the gray monsters. I think he blamed them for all that had happened, that we were out of sight of land and making slow progress. Thrashing about in a frenzy, the voracious creatures swam off in a rush. Segundo, dripping sweat, crawled back on deck, his face flushed. *"Malditos,"* he said, shaking his fist at the fleeing sharks. They did not return that day.

I calculated our noon position to be four degrees north of the equator on May 25. We were riding along longitude 78° W, which put us roughly forty miles from land and sixty miles northwest of Buenaventura, Colombia's leading port city. I held a serious conference with myself, debating whether to head due north for Panama, or to follow a course west from Cabo Marzo across the Gulf of Panama in an effort to follow the favorable currents to the islands of Coiba and Jicarita, and then make for Costa Rica or Nicaragua. From that point I could decide whether to go on to Mexico.

We awakened to another beautiful day marred only by the absence of wind. We were caught in a calm that lasted 24 hours. The air was humid and our clothes stuck to our skins. The barometer fell and kept falling as the sun set with unparalleled splendor. At nightfall flurries of wind came out of the southwest varying from ten to fifteen miles per hour, and we started running a good four to five knots. At 2300 hours the wind increased. Clouds swept over the face of the moon, and a tropical downpour pelted us. I was glad to go off watch an hour later and felt sorry for Segundo when he pulled on his oilskins. He didn't say anything. He just looked at me and went out on deck. The deckhouse was warm and comfortable, and as I lay there listening to the straining balsa and the growing force of the sea and wind, I hoped it would blow over and I could get a good night's rest. I fell asleep to the sound of creakings and groanings as the *Feathered Serpent* climbed and plunged in the heavy seas. At 0300 the full force of the gale hit us, and I was jostled about my bunk wondering what had happened. Segundo stuck his head in the door and shouted for us to come out on deck. Sleepily I crawled into my foul weather gear and hurriedly tied on my life preserver and went outside, the navigator fast behind.

Lost on the High Seas

We were confronted with a howling maelstrom. The sea boiled and the wind nearly took my breath away. Continuous flashes of lightning illuminated the sky and turned the surface of the mountainous water a vivid purple. The sound of the thunder was terrifying. We had no more than set our feet on the deck when a huge breaking wave roared down upon us, and we hung on for dear life. It struck the balsa with a devastating force. She was flung completely about so that her bows pointed south. The sail went aback and we were pushed astern. We all flung ourselves toward the halyard to lower the sail, for fear of becoming dismasted. Before we could lay a hand on the line, we heard a ripping sound and watched helplessly as the sail split apart and started flapping in the screaming wind. The strain on the *Feathered Serpent* was tremendous. A lesser vessel would have foundered.

We managed to reef the tattered sail. The rudder oar was whipping back and forth and we struggled to lash it down. She yawed and pitched, then went glissading down a giant wave into a trough that looked a hundred feet deep. The waves rolled down upon us at terrific speed, threatening to submerge boat and men. But the *Feathered Serpent* would climb to the top. Sometimes a wave would break twenty yards from the balsa and rush toward us like a hissing monster and slam into her side, inundating the vessel with tons of water. We clung to the bamboo in desperation, unable to move under the pressure of the pounding sea, fighting for breath.

The gale continued to howl full strength. We streamed a sea anchor from the stern, and the pull straightened us out as we started to ride, with the wind coming from astern. How we managed to get about in the wind and the sea I will never know. It is difficult to put into words what takes place on shipboard during a gale. My log lists the winds at over 50 miles an hour and the waves 40 feet high. I was afraid we were caught in a hurricane—it was the season. Hurricane winds blow at 75 to 125 miles an hour in these waters.

The brief storm blew itself out at 0430 hours and we found ourselves in a calm. The contrast was startling. Just before it ended I had begun planning what we would do if forced to abandon ship.

With the wind and sea slowly returning to normal, Segundo and I turned in, leaving the navigator alone on deck in a heavy rain. Next morning when I went on watch, the balsa was a shambles. The *Feathered Serpent* had been a beautiful thing the day we departed Salaverry. Her golden color had matched the rays of the sun. Slowly she had changed to a musty gray. The lines were wearing and darkening, and the cane was a dingy gray-black. Fungus had collected in the deckhouse, with green patches hanging in the rafters. Nevertheless, she was clean, with no dirt or grease as on ordinary ships, the deck polished bright by our hands and feet, the wind, the sea, and the sun. Our spare totora bundled up and lashed down on the foredeck had been carried away by the wind, along with line, extra bamboo, and extra wood. The mainsail, upon which we relied, was torn to shreds, and we broke out the Dacron emergency sail and hoisted it on the same yardarm. Bits of string and line, placed about the balsa for general use, were gone. The galley was a wreck. Cutlery, pots, pans, cups, dishes,

The author at the helm. (Photo by Tom Spain, CBS News.)

(Above left) *The navigator as Father Neptune christens Segundo with sea water poured from a gourd after crossing the equator.*

Deadly poisonous sea snake held at pole's length.

(Above) *The* Feathered Serpent *with her three-man crew. (Photo by Tom Spain, CBS News.)*

Fishing with a hand net.

Punta Cruces off the starboard quarter seven hours before the Feathered Serpent *went aground.*

The shoal that claimed the balsa.

The morning after. Sails furled, we float free in the Bay of Octavia on a crippled ship, without hope.

Colombian fishermen come aboard to inspect damage.

(Above) *Canoeman paddles author through dangerous reefs off northern Colombia. (Photo by Segundo Grandez.)*

(Left) *Sea pollution of drift-wood and other floating debris catches eye of helmsman.*

(Above) *Panamanian fishing boat is hailed by Segundo.* (Right) *Peruvian ambassador Guillermo Gerberding-Melgar comes aboard and chats with author in Panama Bay. (Photo by Tom Spain, CBS News.)*

Barnacle-encrusted hulls of the Feathered Serpent *shown as she is lifted out of the water at Manta, Ecuador, just after having crashed into the harbor.*

Detail of broken balsa at Manta.

Maya city of Tikal in the jungles of Guatemala.

The author pauses to take one last look before going ashore, Panama Bay. (Photo by Steven Bailey.)

and assorted pieces were missing. A general inspection showed the radio receiver useless, drenched by the waves that had swept inside the deckhouse during the night. The hurricane lamps were shattered, as were the running lights. Part of the roof of the deckhouse had been torn away. But generally there was no serious damage. We spent the entire day getting things shipshape.

That night there was a halo around the moon, and dark patches of rain clouds streaked across its face in a forbidding way. All day long, large swells rolled in from a lumpy sea. At 2300 hours the wind began blowing from the southwest, and the *Feathered Serpent* labored under the onslaught of greater seas which swept over her stern as she ran before the wind on a northeasterly course. Dazed, we worked through our watches under sheets of solid rain that were beginning to wear us down. There wasn't a dry place in the balsa, and we slept in our oil-skins so as to be ready for any emergency.

For seven long days we were pounded by the elements. In all that time we saw the sun only three times. We didn't know our position but guessed we were being carried by the currents northwest across the Gulf of Panama. The depressing weather and hard work gave me an appetite. I began to take a bowl of fish soup every day. I felt much better for it. On the twenty-seventh the day was fairly calm, with variable winds, but during the night a violent storm came up and huge seas broke over the bow and stern. The leeside of the balsa was continually awash. Our course was 310–320 degrees, except when the wind came out of the west; then we ran with it on a bearing of 45 degrees northeast. It rained almost the entire time. Our clothes were damp. When the wind wasn't blowing, the heat was unbearable. On the twenty-ninth the sea was glassy calm and we were treated to a magnificent sunset that broke through the clouds. The calm lasted through the night and into the next day. It was frustrating sitting on the sea, like a duck in a pond, under a sweltering tropical heat that filtered through the overhanging clouds. We moved about the deck like robots, talking little and sleeping when we were not on watch. On the afternoon of the thirtieth, winds gusted up to thirty miles an hour, bringing large drops of rain. It continued raining for twenty-four hours without letup. It was impossible to keep dry, even with the oil-skins.

The sharks came back, circling the balsa in ever-increasing numbers. We usually ignored them, but when they struck the balsa Segundo and the navigator would become annoyed and drive them off with poles, knives, and the gaff hook. Once Segundo tired of the whole thing and broke out the rocket pistol. He shot a couple of flares that sizzled off a shark's head with a terrific blast of light, smoke, and spray. The shark did not return.

Man Overboard

Early on the morning of the thirty-first, the forty-seventh day of the voyage, I fell overboard while standing watch. It was raining and I was alone at the helm in my bare feet when I slipped off the bamboo deck. Before I could catch myself I plunged into the midst of a school of sharks. My bright yellow rain gear was certain to attract their attention. I could see them moving in my direction as I hit the water. I twisted, bounced off the rudder oar, and landed feet first. I went down to the shoulders, then kicked my legs scissor fashion for dear life, knowing that if I got behind the balsa the sharks would tear me apart. I managed to come up out of the water waist-high and got a hand on the rudder oar. Terror-stricken, I kicked and clawed at the bamboo cane with my free hand. Catching hold,

I pulled myself up on deck like a madman—the image of shark's teeth sinking into my legs and pulling me back gave me extra strength. Frustrated, the sharks lashed about in confusion, searching for their escaped victim. I sat still a long time, letting the rain fall on my face and wondering how I had managed to get back on board.

As the day wore on I climbed to the crow's nest for a look around. There was no sight of land, but my glasses picked up three birds off to the east, lots of driftwood, and a coconut floating on the sea. I estimated we were thirty miles offshore, more of a hunch than anything. What shore, I wasn't certain. But we seemed to be drifting due north. This was good news and canceled out the possibility of our being carried out to the South Pacific. It meant we were drifting along the coast toward Panama Bay. The driving rain forced me to deck. I inspected the totora floats; they seemed to be floating high and dry. Inside the deckhouse I pulled a stem of totora from the thatched roof and squeezed it between my fingers. Water oozed out of the ends. Withdrawing several more samples, I went out on deck and tossed them into the water. Waterlogged as they were, the tiny air capillaries maintained their buoyancy.

On the morning of June 1, our nineteenth day out of Manta, we awoke to discover several forested islands ten miles off the starboard bow. The navigator called us out of the deckhouse and announced we were at the islands of Jicarón, Jicarita, and Coiba off the southwestern coast of Panama, and that we had crossed the gulf. Segundo and I were too excited to question his calculations. On May 28th he had plotted a position of 5° 55′ south, longitude 79° 12′ west. We could have taken the current the 150 miles or so to reach the location he gave in the elapsed time of about four days. Maybe we had misjudged him and he knew what was doing after all. I hoped so, for if the position he gave was accurate we had made a fantastic passage.

After some thought I asked for another position line as the sun was shining. The mountain ranges on the mainland attained a height of 5,115 feet above sea level, and I should have seen them from the crow's nest the day before. According to my reckoning we had been drifting north, not west, and I couldn't figure out how we could be where he indicated.

We laid our sleeping bags out to dry in the sun and washed our stacks of soiled clothing. The sea was a Mediterranean blue and as smooth as a lake. Becalmed as we were, the current pushed us north toward the green islands that looked like isles of paradise to eyes that had not seen land in weeks. It was too much trouble to worry about anything. We were tired. I figured if we failed to sight a fishing boat we could drop anchor and paddle to shore in the rubber dinghy or lash two of the *caballitos* together.

Washing my clothing at the bow between the bowsprits, I watched little black fish with tiny mouths feeding on the newly forming barnacles. They kept the number of the creatures down and we considered them our friends. Friendly, they swam right into my hands and nibbled at the hems of my T-shirts. Schools of purple fish with black stripes down their sides were attracted to my laundry. Golden dorado fish circled about, and minute guppies and jellyfish drifted by. A funny fish with a rust-colored body rippled the surface of the water, raised its head and turned over, showing its yellow belly before disappearing. I kept an eye open for sea snakes, for I was still fearful of the poisonous reptiles working their way into the floats and biting one of us. A shark nosed about the balsa, a magnificent creature attracted to the white material, but it soon swam off.

At 1600 the navigator, after taking another sun fix, reported our position to be the same. Any ideas we had of confirming this vanished when the currents took hold of the balsa and whipped us to the west, away from the islands. Clouds came down around them and they disappeared from view toward the sunset. That night the water was so still you could see the stars reflected in it, something I had never witnessed before. At 2300 hours the wind started to blow again. We took a northwest heading. Right after going off watch I drank a bowl of hot chocolate and turned in.

The following morning rain began to fall from overcast skies, and we coursed north in light airs. Early in the afternoon forested peaks loomed out of the mists. The navigator reported we were off the coast of Costa Rica and nearing Point Burica. This was too good to be true.

A seventy-five-pound green turtle tried to climb aboard, and we played with the "chicken" and pushed it off. But it came right back. Segundo hauled it up on deck with a gaff hook and claimed it for the galley. Shortly after, a sea snake swam up between the stern floats. We thought it would get into the floats. Segundo gave it a swipe with the long bamboo pole, sending up a great splash. It turned as if to attack, glaring at us with hypnotic eyes, then sank from sight.

Aimlessly we drifted north along the forested coastline some fifteen miles offshore. Seeing the jungles brought back nostalgic memories of my explorations, and I longed to set foot on land again. After taking a sun shot at 1730 hours, the navigator confirmed that we were off Point Burica, Costa Rica. The sea was luminous that night, a throbbing series of pulsations from a million glowfish. At 2200 the thing I most feared happened. As I bent down to wash my cup at the stern, after my coca tea, my eyes fell on a yellowish sea snake staring up at me. It had attached itself to the sternsprit. I directed the beam of my flashlight into its eyes. It coiled into a ball and fell back into the sea. When Segundo came on watch I warned him to be on guard against the sea snakes. He listened wide-eyed. When I went inside I heard him fumbling with the lamps to light the ship. He disliked snakes as much as I did. Sure enough, during his watch several tried to swim into the floats. He flung them away with his bamboo pole.

Driftwood

On June 3, the fiftieth day of the voyage and our twenty-first day out of Manta, the wind, which had been very light to flat calm, changed abruptly when the rain arrived and began to freshen from the west as the sea started running. The weather was hot and humid, and with the heavy rain it became unbearable. We worked on deck in our shorts, barefooted, alert for sea snakes, which the navigator kept insisting were eels. The murky sea was dotted with white horses, and we galloped along on a northern course in a world of howling chaos. Around noon we were startled to see torrents of driftwood—whole trees, dislodged from the banks during the recent storm, shot by. Chunks of wood, planks, boards, and tiny islands of earth with small saplings clinging to them swirled about. Later, when the seas calmed, we saw birds feeding on the undersides of planks; we pulled one aboard to see what it was they found so delicious. They had been feeding on tiny crabs. The drifts teemed with yellow-and-black sea snakes. They appeared to be of a different species from those we had seen days before. We stopped examining the drifts.

In late afternoon the drifts were still with us. We had been pushing tree trunks, logs, and large planks away from the balsa ever since a large log had lodged itself between the floats and started thumping up and down. Concerned that it might do some damage, we worked it out by forcing our poles down through the bamboo deck. We were on constant lookout, day and night.

For two days we struggled to keep the driftwood away from the balsa in a boisterous sea. Then the swell eased and the sea turned calm. Wisps of mist sped across the sun; we strained our eyes for sight of land, and just before sunset we thought we saw the top of a forested peak sticking up out of the fog. That night we could discern shore lights eight miles away. We hoped the villagers would spot our colorful sail in the morning and send a boat out to investigate.

Next morning the sun hung low in the east and a great circle of rainbow colors enveloped it, slanting rays of golden light through the peaks. The three of us stared eastward for signs of life but saw only green vegetation. I feared we had been pushed into a nameless bay.

As the day progressed the sun burned off the fog. It grew hot and wisps of vapor rose skyward from the wet totora and rope. The navigator took a sun fix and announced our northward passage since morning to be seven miles. "Rubbish," exulted Segundo, and then, pointing to a rocky pinnacle five miles south of us, turned his back and said, "That rock was off to the right this morning." He was right. I had observed it earlier. With his sharp eyesight and natural instinct for noticing landmarks, Segundo needed no lenses or instruments to tell him in which direction we were traveling. The navigator did not answer. Afterward I jotted down the following lines in the log:

> At 1730 hours many sea snakes approach the balsa. They are attracted to the floats and we are kept busy fending them off with poles. Balsa is shriveling up from dry heat. Ropes very loose and figureheads hanging low. Mast has tilted and one of our Turk's-head weathervanes fell off sometime during night. Stores are spoiling. Oatmeal filled with worms, chocolate damp and flaky, sugar

wet—so are the matches. Kerosene lost overboard during
storm. Using one running light, port. Still not sure of
our position.

Next day I wrote:

Friday, June 6.

1800. Dawn begins with an intense electrical storm. Flashes of
lightning come down from the heavens with a loud
crack, striking very close to balsa. Shafts of light dance
about us with a bang, making our ears ring. Four hours
of rain from 0800 to noon. Day very dark and depressing. Navigator says we are 10 miles south of Salsipuedes,
Costa Rica. Rain stops. Light air followed by calm. Mist
rises from shoreline, revealing a stretch of mountainous
jungle. A chain of high rocks lies south of us, one towering 60 feet, indicating we were pushed south during
night. Yesterday we were three miles north of them.
Barometer drops one point, from 29 to 28. Late afternoon slight breeze blowing from east. We hoist sail and
head seaward in an effort to escape the unknown bay of
swirling currents that take us back and forth like a yo-yo.

As evening came and clouds rolled in about us, Segundo,
with a swing of his bamboo pole, killed a sea snake while it was
nosing about the starboard sternsprit. Carefully he laid it out
on deck for inspection. The navigator, whose curiosity got the
best of him, looked over Segundo's shoulder and gasped when
he saw the beautiful pair of poison fangs laid back by Segundo's
knife. He exclaimed that he would have sworn the swimming
things were eels. Later Segundo skinned the reptile and
stretched it out on a board. He took pains to hang it in the
most conspicuous place on board—on the side of the deckhouse,
next to the entrance, so anyone entering couldn't help noticing

it. It was his trophy, to be sure, but I think he meant it as a reminder to the navigator's fertile imagination. "Eels, indeed," he said, after the job was completed. He stroked his beard and said: "If he ever is fortunate enough to visit the jungle, he'll lose an arm if he mistakes a jaguar for a pussy cat and tries to pet it."

The next day was calm, with variable light airs whiffing in from the southwest, west, and northwest. We awoke to find ourselves exactly where we had been three days before—five to six miles west of a mountain peak. Hampered by large masses of driftwood—from chips of wood to whole trees as much as sixty feet long, which gave the appearance of wrecked schooners with their tall branches sticking up out of the water like masts of a ship—we fought to get into the breeze, light as it was, or into the ebbtide and make for the open sea. But it was no good. The swirling currents held us in a pocket and carried us around in a large circle in and about the unknown bay.

Cabo Marzo

At 0900, Segundo's good eyes spotted a man paddling a dugout canoe parallel to the shore half a mile south of us. We waved and shouted at the tops of our voices to get his attention. Just when we thought he would disappear over the horizon, he turned and started paddling toward us. Standing barefoot on the stern prow, the native, wearing a straw hat and white pants cut off above the knee, propelled his light craft with powerful strokes and was upon us before we knew it. "*Oye, hermano,*" called Segundo, through cupped hands, "*donde estamos?*"

The canoeman, with skin blackened by the sun, stopped his canoe dead in the water thirty yards off our port quarter and eyed us curiously. Segundo queried him again. "Hey, brother, where are we?"

"Cabo Marzo," replied the canoeman in a deep voice that carried across the still water as if spoken through a megaphone.

"Cabo Marzo!" the navigator bellowed. "Which Cabo Marzo?"

"There is only one Cabo Marzo, señor," replied the native paddler. "Cabo Marzo, Colombia."

The navigator sat down on the deck, his face buried in his broad hands. "I am ruined," he said. "Ruined."

For weeks we had observed with interest the navigator taking his sun sights and plotting our position on one chart after the other. The thin pencil line had worked its way along the Colombian coast, across the Gulf of Panama and all the way to Salsipuedes, Costa Rica. We had been ecstatic. Navigational errors had been made in the past, but we were willing to forgive and forget. If what he had said was true, then Mexico would have been a mere fifteen sailing days' distance; and if the hurricanes were late in arriving, we had a good chance of making landfall there. But all our hopes had evaporated like drops of water thrown on a hot skillet. It was as if some mysterious hand had set us back, overnight, five hundred miles to the Colombian coast. Five hundred miles!

Segundo and I stood looking at each other, stunned and disbelieving, shaking our heads. Ever since Manta, when the balsa had plummeted into the harbor, our relationship with the navigator had deteriorated. Segundo doubted he had ever been a navigator, and I was beginning to think our passenger was along strictly for the adventure.

Under normal circumstances we might have been angered by the bad news. As it was, our position did not change the fact that we were stranded in a bay. After the initial shock and disappointment wore off, where we were, or where the navigator thought we were, became unimportant. It was almost a humorous situation because of the fuss that had been made over the importance of having a navigator aboard. The charts showed us to be in the Bahia Octavia, one of the most inhospitable and current-ridden inlets along the entire Colombian coast. Currents are so strong that lightly powered boats have great difficulty in making headway against them, which explained why we had seen such large amounts of driftwood. A waterlogged, drift-type balsa raft had very little chance of ever getting out of the bay on its own. We might just as well have been caught in a giant whirlpool five miles in diameter.

The currents and trade winds had carried us north along the coast just as I had predicted. Even our attempt to get across the Gulf of Panama had proved fruitless. The current had pushed us east toward the continent, not west as planned. I decided we should bide our time and wait for a strong offshore wind to get out of the bay. Then we could get into the current and head north; the object was to keep from being set ashore by the northwesterly winds. Navigation would be by dead reckoning. Never again did the navigator attempt celestial navigation. The sextant and other instruments were put away under the bunk, where they remained for the rest of the voyage.

Breaking Up on the Rocks

The remainder of the day proved uneventful until 2300 hours. I was at the helm steering west-northwest in a light breeze that blew at a steady seven knots, yet found we were drawing dangerously close to shore. The tide was running, and there must have been a southerly set to the current, for we were being pushed southeast: what we gained to windward we lost to the current. I called out to the men to help me bring the balsa about in order to take advantage of the currents. While we were doing this the sea began to roil and the wind started gusting from the west. Walls of water beat against our starboard side, pushing us closer to land. No matter what we tried, the *Feathered Serpent* failed to answer the helm. She was being drawn to the rocky shore.

Since the wind was blowing directly onto the land, we decided to put out the two sea anchors so as to keep away from the pounding surf until the tide and the weather changed. We rigged one of the sea anchors with drogues. While we were doing this, I looked over my shoulder at the roaring surf breaking against the cliffs of the shoreline. To be driven onto the rocks would be certain destruction. Never in my life had I seen such a malevolent stretch of coastline. The swells burst against the black cliffs and shot high into the inky darkness. I tried to imagine how we would save ourselves if the balsa ran ashoal. There was no way for swimmers to get ashore, because the cliffs rose up out of the water like walls. The tropical vegetation was a good forty feet above the sea. Compared to this situation, the breakers of Talara seemed like a picnic. There we could have surfed over the breakers and beached the balsa. Here it was a matter of saving not the balsa but our lives.

By 0100 the balsa began to veer toward shore as if pulled by a magnet. We were making every effort to get around Punta Cruces, the southernmost end of the bay, and into the Gulf of Cupica (a good ten by twenty miles), which would give us space to operate. But it was no good. By 0115 we were caught in a vicious surf no more than three hundred yards offshore.

I ordered Segundo to get the rubber life raft and emergency radio, and then dashed inside the deckhouse, making a mental list of what was needed. There was a chance of survival, and if we managed to get ashore we would need a wide range of supplies, my precious film and cameras, along with identification papers and traveler's checks. There was little time, but I tried not to forget the important things we would need later.

Dragging the stores out on deck, I helped Segundo inflate the dinghy, and when it was blown up we lashed it to the stern and started filling it, lashing down everything in plastic bags. We were shocked to see that it was only a two-man raft, not the four-man I had ordered. No matter; it would hold our emergency gear.

We had been so intent on filling the dinghy with stores that we had not looked up, and when we did we saw a terrifying sight. The *Feathered Serpent* was unmanageable, the slamming surf curling around her and the cliffs no more than a hundred yards away. The navigator had gone forward and was staring in the direction of the shore as if hypnotized. I called to him but he did not reply. Worse, we were bearing down on a cluster of lava-colored reefs between us and the cliffs. Segundo was at the helm, working it back and forth to give us some propulsion. I scrambled forward and threw out the kedge anchor, hoping one of its bills would catch on the hard bottom and keep us away from the reef. I payed out thirty yards, then made the rode, or anchor cable, fast to the forward mooring bit. It did catch, for at fifty yards or less from the reef the balsa swung around in a half-circle and held, her stern pointing to the rocks. The sound of the surf breaking against the cliffs was frightening, and we tried not to think about the breaking of the rode.

The anchor held us until 0300. Then the rode broke. We shot forward toward the reef. I grabbed a bamboo pole from the deck and flung it toward Segundo. "Try to hold her off!" I shouted, grabbing another one and sliding it down the deck in the direction of the navigator. He looked at it and shook his head. "I am not going to have one of those things driven through me like a stake," he yelled, refusing to pick it up. There was no use arguing. I snatched one of the spare halyards and went to the stern to join Segundo. When we got close enough we laid the ends of the poles on the rocks and pushed with all our might. We were two men attempting to hold back six or seven tons driven by the raging elements. The sea, breaking in giant cataracts over the raft, lifted her up and smashed her down into one of the reefs. We were stranded.

We could feel the balsa shudder as the sea began to punish her. Chunks of totora were torn out of her. I saw the lower half of one of the centerboards float away. Rocking back and forth, we could hardly keep our footing. The sea boiled around us, and the *Feathered Serpent* seemed to be in a death spasm. Had she been an ordinary vessel she would have foundered and sunk. It didn't seem possible that we could survive in the swirling waters against the sheer cliffs, with only a flimsy raft to protect us. But I elected to stick with the *Feathered Serpent*. She was a lucky ship, and somehow I believed we would escape. It was a risk, but one we had to take.

I cannot describe the horror of the next three hours. We tried everything imaginable to get off, but we were imprisoned on the reef as surely as if we were part of it. The sea remained lumpy, throwing us about and hitting us hard. Pieces of bamboo floated to the surface, crushed under the weight of the balsa and the thrashing sea. It was a dark, gloomy night, and we were drenched with spray. I was sick with worry and despair, afraid we were going to be pounded to pieces. A little before 0500 a faint off-shore breeze came up, as if by a miracle—usually it blew only during the night, if at all, and even then too weakly to be of use. But this morning it was stronger. In the half-light we could see the sail flutter. A large wave hit us, the balsa careened to starboard, and we were off the reef. There was hope.

"Check the sea anchors!" I shouted to the navigator. "Cut the lines!"

I grabbed the mainsheet and Segundo took the helm. Fortunately, the rudder oar was still in one piece. The sail filled, then emptied and fell slack. I shouted to Segundo, "Port! Hard to port!"

"You mean starboard?" he shouted back.

"Hard over to port. Quick!"

Segundo ignored my order and threw the helm hard to starboard. Thanks to his quick thinking the *Feathered Serpent* came back into the wind. The navigator lumbered up and said he had cut the lines to the sea anchors. The sail filled once more and we started to creep away from the reef. Slowly at first, then faster. The tide had changed and we were being carried north. It was an incredible stroke of luck. I slapped Segundo across the shoulders. "Good work," I said in Spanish. He had been right and I wanted him to know it. He flashed his white teeth in a smile that reached from ear to ear as he tapped my arm with his left hand.

Fifty yards from the reef our forward progress came to an abrupt end. We wheeled 180 degrees and then headed back the way we had come. Something was holding us up. I raced around the balsa looking for the cause and spotted a white line five feet below the surface of the water off the starboard quarter. A line to one of the sea anchors had fouled on the bamboo deck and was hung up on a rock. I tried to reach it but couldn't get my knife on it. Segundo dashed forward and threw himself into the water head first. I managed to grab one of his legs and hold on. We had to hurry. The swirling waters were taking us back toward the ripsaw reef. He cut the line and I hauled him aboard. We hastened back to the helm and got the balsa back into the wind. She limped along, and by 0600 we were five miles north of the Point, safely away from the wicked reef, a good five miles offshore.

Our delight at being free from the reef was colossal. Everyone was wet and sleepy, exhausted from the night's work, but that did not matter. We whooped for joy and shouted our thanks to God. Our bright companion, the sun, burned through the mists to sweep the bleakness of night away. As the sun grew hotter, the clouds lifted to expose a jungle shoreline of forested peaks and a long golden beach on which the sea rolled gently. The transformation was spectacular. It was like a scene from a movie of the South Pacific Islands. We wouldn't have been surprised to see hula dancers on the beach and outriggers coming out to welcome us.

Nobody came. We saw no trace of life. Then the realization dawned on us that we were standing on a broken vessel, a hulk of broken reeds and twisted bamboo. Every shudder of the balsa communicated itself to us through our feet. We were lucky to be alive, much less afloat, but the *Feathered Serpent* would never carry us to Panama or anywhere else. She was finished.

———◆———

Ghost Ship

Colombian Adventure

In all the excitement, I hadn't noticed that the weight of the stores had been too much, and the whole middle section of the dinghy was awash. We hauled it aboard and found a good deal of the precious cargo ruined. Lost to the expedition were two 16mm motion-picture cameras—a Bolex and a Bell & Howell loaned by CBS. I should have put them in buckets of fresh water and kept them submerged until I could get to a camera repair shop, but I did not know this at the time. Next day they were corroded from the briny water and frozen tight.

My own Nikons were saturated with sea water. They had served me faithfully over the years; it was like losing my eyes. I had felt certain the plastic bags and silica gel would keep them dry. I also lost a 200mm telephoto lens, a 21mm wide-angle, and a 50mm lens. Fortunately, my two waterproof Nikonos cameras came through all right, and I managed to salvage one side of my binoculars by washing it out with fresh water, which gave me a monocular for future use.

Checking a can of exposed motion-picture film, I was horrified to discover it filled with sea water. I stripped the sealing tape away from one can after another and found twenty-four hundred-foot rolls soaking wet. In all, I lost 2,400 feet of irreplaceable film. It took me hours to get over the shock. I had worked countless hours photographing important events since leaving Manta; this loss was far greater than the cameras. While the laboratory later managed to salvage some footage, the greater part was lost forever. Again I had made the error of not keeping them in a canister of fresh water, which doesn't seem to harm exposed motion-picture film.

By noon we had almost everything worth salvaging laid out on the deck, drying in the sun. The balsa was drifting slowly northward toward a cluster of rocks rising out of the sea. I figured we would reach them in a day or two unless the currents took us south again. The *Feathered Serpent* was a floating wreck, but I didn't want to make her a derelict by abandoning her. Segundo had spotted smoke earlier in the day, which meant a native hut was located somewhere in the jungle. If we could reach it and get help, we might be able to tow the balsa into a safe harbor. So I decided to paddle ashore with Segundo and leave the navigator to guard the balsa until we could get back to it. If the balsa got dangerously close to the rocky pinnacles, he was instructed to lash the two *caballitos* together and row ashore. He was to wait for us on the beach and, if we didn't make contact within forty-eight hours, to fire off a red flare every three hours until we found him.

As soon as Segundo learned we were going ashore, he started whittling paddles out of the extra figureheads with his machete. The serpent heads served as broad blades, and he soon rounded the ends into handles. I took a hand compass, two cans of pineapple juice, a knife, a waterproof flashlight, six extra batteries, a large bar of chocolate, and a canteen of water and stuffed them into a watertight bag and lashed it to the rubber dinghy. I put a small bag of coca leaves, a waterproof cylinder of matches, and a candle into a plastic bag and shoved them into my shirt pockets, closing the flaps with a safety pin. I slipped traveler's checks and our identification papers into a waterproof money belt and tied the belt around my waist. Then I inflated the dinghy with the hand pump. When Segundo had finished shaping the paddles, I attached a line to the handgrip of the machete and tied it to the safety line around the dinghy. With that, we were ready to depart.

Saying our farewells, we pushed off, leaving the navigator alone at the stern. I was at the bow of the dinghy and Segundo took the stern position. Had there been any natives watching us from ashore, they would have seen two wild-looking bearded men, wearing straw hats, paddling toward them in a fury. Wielding red-and-white serpent figureheads and riding a bright yellow, rubber dinghy, which appeared like a golden boat when seen from afar, we might have been mistaken for the returning Bochica, as the Feathered Serpent was known by ancient Colombians, with the larger rainbow-colored balsa riding the waves behind us.

The beach, broad on the port bow, was a good five miles away. We pointed the little dinghy to a pair of small quays topped with vegetation. It is easy to misjudge distances at sea, but I estimated they were five or six miles south of the beach. We took an oblique course, which meant we had about seven or eight miles to cover before darkness.

The sea heaved gently, but we seemed to be paddling against a strong current, and we feared being swept out to sea. As the hours passed, however, we could see we were putting distance between us and the balsa, and by three o'clock in the afternoon we could no longer see it when we dipped into the small troughs. By four it was gone entirely, even when we reached the crests and looked for it over our shoulders.

We paddled in tandem, changing from side to side to keep a straight and steady course. The sun was hot; we could feel it burning the backs of our necks, and the sweat trickled down our backs as we paddled. My arms were tired, and every half-hour or so we rested a few minutes. My legs hurt, for they were curled up under me, cutting off the circulation. I could not change places with Segundo, whose legs were stretched out on either side, without flipping the dinghy. We had seen many sea snakes swimming by and did not want to risk snakebite by falling into the sea.

At seven o'clock we navigated the boiling sea between the rocky islets and ran for an inlet a mile or so ahead. At the mouth, we rode the heaving swells like surfboarders. We had all we could do to keep the rubber raft from turning over. Once inside the natural harbor, I was for putting in to the rocky shore a bare hundred yards off the starboard beam; the dinghy would have made a shelter, and we had food for the night. But Segundo was against it; he wanted to make for the native hut he said was not far away.

"I smell smoke," he shouted against the roar of the breakers. "Why sleep with the tigers when we can spend the night under a dry roof?"

"It's getting dark," I yelled back over my shoulder. "It's safer to put in while we can. We'll never find that hut in the dark."

He shouted back at me: "You leave that to me! Paddle harder!"

My arms ached, my legs were numb—I wasn't capable of paddling another hour.

"Rest a minute," said Segundo, sensing the pain in my legs.

"It's really safer to put in here," I hollered. "Come on. I'm all right."

"*Carajo!*" thundered my companion. The tone of his voice startled me. "There's a hut in there!" Tempers had flared over the weeks, and we were all sick of seeing one another, yet Segundo and I had a common bond which even the elements couldn't break. Only the certainty of that hut would have made him speak that way.

"Okay!" I yelled back. "Let's go."

We started paddling with renewed energy, and at eight o'clock, when it was getting dark, we felt the paddles hit the soft sand under the raft. We clambered over the side and manhandled the raft toward the beach. I nearly fell as my feet hit the bottom, and it was all I could do to keep my cramped legs from buckling under me. Staggering through the gentle swells, we ran the dinghy up on the beach and moored it to a bush fifty yards from the water. The land danced before our eyes, but our gladness at being safe ashore was enough to make us swagger around, slapping each other on the back, with the rain running down our faces. I opened the bag with the provisions and we celebrated by sharing a can of pineapple juice. A flash of lightning illuminated the beach and thunder rumbled overhead. It was time to get moving. Segundo, with the flashlight in one hand and the machete in the other, led the way. "Come on," he said, throwing the bag over his shoulder. I tottered right behind, exuberant with good will and ready to follow him through the jungle unquestioningly. I was beginning to feel more confident now that we were on land.

We negotiated a sandy swamp and found ourselves in a thicket, where Segundo picked up a pig trail running off into the jungle. We tramped along for half an hour with the rain splattering on the canopy of leaves overhead. The jungle was quiet, as always during a downpour. Suddenly I heard a pig grunt, and much to my surprise I discovered we were standing under a hut built on stilts. Looking up, I saw a light shining through the cracks of the floor and heard a woman laugh, then a child cry.

"*Buenas noches, señora*," said Segundo, stepping out into

the rain so that the occupants of the house could see him. I wondered what they thought when they looked down and saw a black-bearded figure with a wide-brimmed hat, looking for all the world like Captain Kidd, standing in their front yard with a bearded blond companion, both dripping wet. A woman stuck her head out the door and came out on the porch with a candle.

"Who are you?" she asked.

Like an old merchant ready for his first customer, Segundo rubbed his hands, bowing from the waist and doing a little jig with his feet—a habit he displayed whenever he met a woman of any age for the first time. It looked a little odd but had devastating results. He quickly told our story.

"Oh!" she exclaimed after he had finished. "You are the ones we have seen sailing back and forth for nearly a week. We thought you were a fishing boat. Come in."

At her remark Segundo stuck a friendly elbow into my ribs. "Come on."

We climbed a shaky ladder made of tree limbs and were suddenly inside a warm room, looking at a middle-aged woman. She called to a young woman sitting on a matted floor, roasting bananas over a fire. Two children, a boy and a girl, sat beside her, staring wide-eyed at the strangers who had interrupted their evening meal. We introduced ourselves, and the lady of the house said her husband was away but would return in the morning; we were welcome to spend the night and to share in their simple fare. We were each given a change of garb—dry pants and shirt taken from a clothesline. We changed in the back room and joined them on the floor, where we ate a meal of boiled snails and baked bananas. It was the most delicious meal of my life and I had no difficulty swallowing, a fact which surprised me as much as the miracle of our good fortune.

Like a storyteller of old, Segundo told of our adventures, all the while drawing the scrumptious little snails from their shells with a needle and popping them into his mouth. When the pile of shells before us reached gigantic proportions and we were given cups of black coffee and tiny sweet bananas— crêpes suzette wouldn't have tasted better—Segundo told her that the third member of the expedition was still out there, somewhere in the bay. "Poor man," said the woman, "alone out there tonight. My husband will find him tomorrow."

"Don't fret, señora. He is well sheltered and has an abundance of food and water. Besides," said my companion, his hypnotic black eyes glowing, "he may not be there tomorrow." When the woman said she didn't understand, he replied, "Our friend has a magic box. When the sun comes up tomorrow morning he will look into it and put himself in Costa Rica or some other place, far away from here." Then he leaned over and whispered in my ear: "It's possible, you know."

With the rain tapping a staccato beat on the thatched roof, we slept on a paper-thin mattress of cotton spread on the floor, inside a cubicle made of mosquito netting.

Shortly after sunrise, when we had changed into our own clothing and eaten a breakfast of baked bananas and coffee, the master of the house returned. He was as affable as his wife and listened to our story with rapt interest. Afterward, he agreed to take us from Chajreda, which was the name of this village, north by canoe to a man who owned large dugout canoes equipped with outboard motors. If anyone could help us, that man could. He promised to have us there by early afternoon. We said our good-byes to the señora, thanking her for her hospitality. We had nothing to give her, least of all Colombian money, and the traveler's checks would have been worthless to her. I gave the children a good-luck chain and charm, promising to send something back with her husband. In a land famous for its good coffee, she asked for a can of Nescafé, of all things. We promised her a large can and departed.

We walked down a tree-covered path to the river and climbed aboard an eighteen-foot dugout canoe. Our host jumped atop a platform which flared at the stern and, with deft strokes of a hardwood paddle, took us away from Chajreda, downriver and out through the surf into the open sea, where we ran parallel with the coast for two hours. It was an exciting ride, what with the sea running barely two inches below the gunwale and water trickling in through cracks in the bottom. When we were not bailing water, we were holding on for dear life, afraid to move for fear of tipping the round-bottomed craft.

When our canoeman beached the dugout at a rocky point to drink from a freshwater stream, he asked if we wanted to go on by sea to Aguacate, our destination, or walk through the jungle. Segundo glanced into the thick vegetation and asked how long it would take. He was informed either way was a journey of four or five hours. "I'm all for the jungle," said my companion. "Take the canoe if you want; I've had enough." Itching to get my feet on solid ground again, I sided with Segundo, and after hiding the dugout in a clump of bushes, we clambered over the rocks and entered the greenery, led by our Colombian guide.

It was exhilarating to be back on the trail again. I drew strength from the earth and filled my lungs with the scented air that only the jungle produces. Huge butterflies wafted by and songbirds warbled their melodies. Tramping along, I caught myself kicking the dirt with my feet in search of pottery fragments. The entire western coast of Colombia is, for the most part, archaeologically unknown; and I longed to start cutting through the jungles toward the country of Dabeiba, less than a hundred miles away, once ruled by a lord who built a great temple with a golden roof which has never been found.

We hurried along and about noon came out to a long strip of white beach lined with palm trees. We took off our shoes and let the hot, dry sand run through our toes. We ate lunch in a small thatched hut under the waving palms where a friend of our guide gave us fruit, coconut, and coffee. After that, we took a trail into the forest, and a two-hour brisk walk brought us to the edge of the jungle. There before us stretched a recently cleared airstrip. I couldn't have been more surprised if it had been Kennedy International Airport. Our guide pointed his finger to a wooden one-story building painted white, two hundred yards away, and said, "Aguacate," then walked us down the muddy field.

Minutes later we were ushered up a short flight of stairs into the house by a husky dark fellow dressed only in shorts and a straw hat. We might easily have taken him for one of those wild Colombian bandits one reads so much about in the newspapers, had it not been for the semi-elegant surroundings in which we found ourselves. A moment later, a short, lean, wiry man about forty years of age, dressed in white slacks, a T-shirt, and white tennis shoes, appeared from inside the house. We shook hands. He wore a pair of dark-framed sunglasses, and I saw his thick eyebrows arch when our guide told him we were one American and one Peruvian stranded in Colombian waters. He asked for our names and papers. After inspecting our passports, he invited us to sit down. He introduced himself as Paraieo Eden, administrator of a newly constructed fishing resort for wealthy fishermen. Our good fortune seemed boundless. To have saved the balsa and our lives was more than enough to expect from fate; but to have come across a fishing resort with an airstrip, in a remote region of Colombia, where there are hardly any roads to speak of and where the villages are few and far between, was better luck than anyone could expect.

While we were talking, an elderly woman with graying hair and dark skin brought in a tray of crackers, cheese, and black coffee, placing it on a small wooden table. She smiled and retired into the kitchen through a swinging door. Señor Eden listened with interest when we told him about the expedition and the events that had brought us to Colombia. He described the dangers of the bay into which we had been pushed and said that the currents often whipped small boats, attempting to sail west, back to the Colombian coast. When he learned that the balsa was still adrift in the bay with a third man, he dispatched a forty-foot dugout equipped with a fifty-horsepower outboard motor and crew to tow it into the harbor.

The *Feathered Serpent* was moored to a buoy two hundred yards from the resort. The crew had found the balsa adrift at the far end of the Bay of Octavia. The day before, local watermen had spotted the strange-looking watercraft and paddled out in their canoes to investigate. Seeing that it was in danger of running aground, they devised an old-type anchor made of half a dozen large rocks independently attached to the line. Once the anchor was on the bottom, the drag effect kept the balsa from drifting farther. The villagers kept the navigator company until he was picked up by the crewmen, which hadn't been any too soon as far as he was concerned, for he had nearly been bitten on the hand by a sea snake while putting out the anchor. It seems he was in a belt of sea snakes that swarmed around the craft as it drifted back and forth in the lower half of the bay very close to shore.

Señor Eden suggested that we speak with his boat crews, who knew the coastline and the nature of the currents as far as Panama Bay. In the meantime, he said, he would extend the hospitality of the resort to us for three days, after which he must leave for the interior and make his report of the death of the owner. Beyond that, he could do nothing. While the arrangements were being made for our lodging, the navigator was brought in to give his report on the whereabouts and the condition of the *Feathered Serpent*. We ate an early dinner and turned in for the night.

Next morning Segundo and I talked to the boat crews, who lived in a cluster of thatched bamboo huts down the road from the resort. Good-natured folk, they invited us inside their cramped quarters for black coffee and told us that from Punta Garachiné the currents swept into Panama Bay, and once we got our vessel into the currents, we would be carried along as if by a river. The hundred miles or so to the point would give us trouble, however, because of the cross-currents, whirlpools, and onshore winds. The situation was going from bad to worse.

We hurried back to the resort building and asked Señor Eden for a canoe so that we could examine the *Feathered Serpent*. He was most obliging, and a half-hour later we were on board the balsa. She was in poor shape. The A-shape mast was wobbly and the deck platform was out of alignment—even worse than after the drop from the crane in the marina at Manta. Both centerboards were gone, broken off under the hulls when the balsa was stranded on the reefs. The cane floats were a mess, cracked and broken, with little if any buoyancy left. But the totora floats were intact, save for a few missing pieces torn out at the bow and stern sections. It was remarkable. The bamboo bundles and fenders had protected the fragile totora. This gave me an idea.

"What say we cut off the cane bundles and try to ride the current to Panama Bay?" I said. "From there we can pick up dugouts and go on to Mexico—if the weather holds out." The idea was to clip the canoes under the deck to compensate for the buoyancy we had lost.

There was a long silence while Segundo walked slowly around the balsa, thinking. I didn't know what else to suggest. Panama Bay, less than 250 miles away, was our only hope. If we could get the *Feathered Serpent* to Panama, my theory that Viracocha had used this sea route and emerged in Central America as Quetzalcoatl, as opposed to the idea that he had sailed to the Pacific Islands, would be substantiated, or at least strengthened.

"Why not?" said Segundo, moving the rudder oar back and forth.

"Can you cut off the cane and make her shipshape?" I asked.

"Give me two days. But how do we get her out of the bay?"

"Señor Eden may help with one of the canoes and an outboard motor."

"Won't we be criticized? The ancients didn't have outboards," he said.

"No, but they had rowers and plenty of canoes. We haven't time to look for fifty canoemen. The object is to put the balsa into the current. The means we use to get out of here is incidental. If we manage to reach Panama Bay on our own, considering our damaged condition, we will have achieved the impossible."

Señor Eden agreed to our plan. He had taken a keen interest in the expedition and said he was privileged to help. We were promised a large dugout with two outboards, and a four-man crew. That afternoon, we retrieved the rubber inflatable at Chajreda and dropped in for a visit with our two lady friends. They received our gift with thanks—a large can of Nescafé and several sea bass we had caught along the way. We were repaid with an invitation to stay for a lunch of fish stew seasoned with coconut juice. We had a wonderful time and remained until the sun disappeared into the ocean.

The next day was devoted to cutting away the cane bundles and getting the balsa ready for the voyage. She rode low in the water, but not so low as we had anticipated, and we were quite pleased. The A-frame mast was straightened, and we onloaded stores including fresh water, stalks of bananas, scores of coconuts and fresh fruit stored in baskets made of raffia. It was hard work at 106 degrees in the sun. Clothing was washed and dried, and at five o'clock on the afternoon of June 11 we were ready to depart the Bahía de Octavia.

We thanked everyone for his help and, with our few belongings perched atop our heads, waded out through the surf to the waiting canoe. Our plan was simple enough. The canoe would tow us out beyond the rocks of Cabo Marzo at least five miles from the shoreline, well into the current, and escort us for twenty-four hours. We would conduct our own trials and see what the *Feathered Serpent* could do in her poor condition. We had no way of knowing what she was capable of, but I figured our escort was good insurance against the possibility of our being pushed into the Bahía de Humboldt, just north of us, or going aground while learning her new sailing characteristics. Save for the loss of her centerboards and a few nicks here and there, the *Feathered Serpent* was pretty much the same vessel that had left Salaverry fifty-nine days before . . . that is, if you didn't look too close. Once we were on our own, we would drift with the current into the Bay of Panama, God willing.

Riding the Currents into Panama Bay

The hours spent with our escort were not without incident. South of Cabo Marzo, on the first day, we dropped the lines as the sun was sinking to observe the effects of the currents. The wild waters would have carried us into the base of a rocky pinnacle had we not put out a line to the waiting canoe. We did not try that again until we were well out to sea. That was the morning of the twelfth. We dropped the lines, hoisted the sail, and sat back to see what the balsa would do in a five-knot light breeze from the southwest. The *Feathered Serpent* veered to starboard, came about, and started circling like a spinning top. We found the cause to be two eighteen-foot bamboo canes dragging underneath, acting like two sweep oars. They had somehow got tangled up when we had cut away the cane bundles. The men, led by Segundo, dived under the balsa and cut them free while the crew kept their eyes peeled for the sea snakes that were all over the place. After that she sailed fairly well until the wind dropped away and we were becalmed. We drifted along with the canoe in attendance. Invariably the *Feathered Serpent* would drift shoreward; when we got within three miles of the coast, we were taken in tow again and pulled farther out into the slow-moving current which flowed north-ward at a steady two miles an hour. All in all, we made fairly good progress until the dugout prepared to leave at midnight on the twelfth. We were sorry to see our guardians depart, but they were running short of gasoline. As it was, they had nursed their gasoline so as to remain with us an extra twelve hours. Upon reflection, I don't know what we would have done without them that day and two nights while we were working out the kinks in the balsa. As the dugout pulled away, we heard one of the crewmen yell to us through cupped hands: "Be careful of Punta Caracoles! The whirlpools are dangerous and will put you ashore! Watch for the current off Punta Garachiné. You will see it. Get inside and you will fly to Panama!" With that, the roar of the motor faded to a purr, and they were gone.

We passed a lonely night drifting in a calm, barely moving. Panama seemed a thousand miles away.

Friday, June 13, the sixtieth day of the voyage and our second day out of Aguacate, we crept along the shoreline in light airs, propelled by a slow current. The words from "The Rime of the Ancient Mariner" which I had learned as a youth—"And all the boards did shrink"—came to me as the *Feathered Serpent* burned under the tropical sun. The ropes loosened and we felt the bamboo deck rocking under our feet like the wooden slats of an old suspension bridge. The *Feathered Serpent* acquired a novel and lumpy motion, but the totora kept her high and dry.

That night we saw the 3,740-foot peak of Garachiné loom up out of the darkness as if about to fall on us, and we had to lift our heads to see the summit against the starlit sky. Then the wind dropped away completely and we were becalmed. There was no doubt about it: We would go aground before we got around the point. Afraid to sleep, the three of us remained on watch in anticipation of the sad ending destiny seemed to have in store for us.

At first light on the morning of the fourteenth, the shoreline appeared out of the darkness like an inky stretch of black sand, then changed to iridescent colors as the rising sun came up over the jungled mountains. We blinked in the bright light and calculated how long it would be before we went aground. We could hear the roar of the breakers less than half a mile away. I guessed we would be on the beach before noon, maybe sooner. An entry in my log that morning reads: "This may be the last day of the expedition. We have been searching for the current, but it has escaped us. Maybe my theories are all wrong. Whatever, we are not going to give up without effort. If we are beached, we have pledged to wait for the tide and try to get the balsa back to sea again; or if that fails, seek help from the Choco Indians of Darién, who have excellent dugout canoes."

"Mira! Mira!" The cry came from the masthead. Segundo was on lookout. *"La corriente!"*

We turned to see a riverlike stream, five hundred yards off the port beam, moving rapidly northward between us and the open sea. It was running so swiftly as to create whitecaps, almost like rapids. The flow carried a chain of debris stretching as far as the eye could see—driftwood, tree trunks, logs. Upon examination with my monocular, I could see a large metal boiler and several Japanese-type glass fishing floats, scraps of colorful plastic containers, bottles, toys, and an odd assortment of items discarded by our "pollution-conscious" society, including several plaited reed baskets tossed away by the Indians. How such a variety of junk had found its way into the current I shall never know. Tall and stately pelicans, their long bills lowered to half-mast, rode the caravan looking for the little silvery anchovies swimming about the drift in huge schools. The sea snakes were there too, in countless numbers, like maggots on a piece of rotting flesh. I had never expected to see anything like it on the voyage.

Then, to our surprise, we felt the balsa move away from the shore toward the "floe." The *Feathered Serpent* trembled as the current took hold of her. The balsa, now out of control, turned a full ninety degrees as if held by a powerful hand and ran with the current, which was as strong and swift as the tributaries of the Amazon on which I had rafted many times. We were stunned by its primeval savagery. I had often laughed at the phrase "Great White River," used to describe the Peruvian current. I shall never do so again.

A half-hour later we were firmly established in the center of the floe, flying along like a sea bird at a speed we hadn't known since the Gulf of Guayaquil, even though we had absolutely no control over the rudder oar and the balsa had her port beam full into the south wind. It was fantastic.

Punta Garachiné faded from sight as we angled past the Bay of San Miguel and entered the Gulf of Panama. It was hard to believe the Atlantic Ocean was barely seventy-five miles to the east of us. Isla del Rey, the largest island in the Archipelago de las Perlas, came into view early in the afternoon, and we hoped to stay between it and the land to avoid being carried back by the strong currents moving in the opposite direction.

That night we saw the glow from Panama against a brilliant electrical display and roars of thunder. We stood for hours just looking at the lights. Around midnight, the balsa took a course between Punta Cocas and the lighthouse situated on the tiny island of Galera. We were still at the mercy of the current. We were amazed at the manner in which we were swept in and out between the islands without being put ashore.

We continued on, with dive-bombing birds hitting the sea around us and large tuna swimming between the floats. Standing watch was a joy, since the sail was furled at the yardarm and the current was doing all the work. It took us east, away from the islands, in the direction of Punta Brujas, and that night we kept on in company with a fleet of fishing boats. The sea was calm.

The following morning we ran northwest, parallel with the land, past a small island, and at 1100 were within sight of Old Panama. Shortly after this we hailed a fishing boat which took us in tow and left us at the entrance of Panama Bay. A motor patrol boat came out and towed us to a spot in front of the Presidential Palace. We were at anchor. It was 1730 on Tuesday, June 17, 1969, the sixty-fourth day of the voyage; we had sailed from Peru to Central America over a sea route I contended could have been used by a wandering sage known as the Feathered Serpent.

"*Dios mío, qué corriente!*" said Segundo, cleating a second mooring line to a buoy. A small motor launch came alongside to clear us with the local authorities. We stepped aboard. "Imagine. Over two hundred and fifty miles in seven days on the upper arm of the Peruvian current without sail. It's a dream come true," said Segundo. "A lot of people wouldn't believe it."

"I don't believe it myself," said the navigator. He had taken the sextant, kept in a wooden box, and put it under his arm.

"Keep it," I said. "As a memento of the expedition. A gift."

He looked at me and blinked. "Thanks."

We were all friends now. The voyage was over. This is the way I had wanted it. I glanced over at the *Feathered Serpent*. There were gulls about the balsa and a large crowd of curiosity-seekers on the wharf. The balsa looked tired and worn. I felt a pang of melancholy and was sad to leave her. In spite of everything, I couldn't imagine her life ending this way. She seemed to be straining at her mooring lines, almost as if she were eager to be on her way again.

Now we put-putted up the wharf amdist the shouts of the spectators. We threw our duffel bags over our shoulders and made our way up the ramp toward the customs office. Later I drafted a cable to CBS News in New York.

Ten days later I put Segundo and the navigator on a plane for Peru. I had hoped to continue the voyage to Mexico, but the hurricane season was full upon us. Strong winds from the Caribbean were blowing over the Isthmus, making the route too dangerous. I hoped to slip a pair of dugouts under the deck platform and continue in late November or early December.

In the meantime, the Peruvian ambassador in Panama had agreed to watch over the balsa while the expedition continued overland to Guatemala, Honduras, and Mexico. Riding safely at anchor, the *Feathered Serpent* faced an interesting test in the months ahead. If she survived that, then she could sail any-where. Perhaps I was asking too much of a great vessel, but it didn't seem right, somehow, to let her languish ignobly on the beach. As a precaution, I authorized the ambassador to put her on a ship and return her to Peru for exhibition if she showed any sign of breaking up.

In the Lands of Quetzalcoatl

So, with the *Feathered Serpent* riding at anchor in Panama Bay, I resumed my investigations, first at the magnificent ruins of Copán in the jungles of Honduras, then on to Tikal in Guatemala and the Pyramids at Teotihuacán in Mexico. Everywhere I noted the murals depicting the Feathered Serpent. The circular building of Calixtlahuaca caught my interest, for it was believed to have been dedicated to the Feathered Serpent —Quetzalcoatl. Its circular design echoed that of the Cloud People of Chachapoyas, who built round buildings dedicated to their own version of this hero-god. But the Mexicans had their "cloud people," too: the Miztecs and the Zapotecs who erected the beautiful monuments of Monte Alban and Mitla which reminded me in many ways of similar temple buildings in Peru. Here, too, I found traces of the legendary figure.

In the land of the Maya, I revisited sites I had studied years before: Palenque, Chichén Itzá, Uxmal, Labna. Everywhere there were signs of Kukulcan. All along the way I investigated evidence of sea trade with the south, from the seafaring Chontal Maya on the Gulf of Mexico to the Highland Maya on the Pacific side of Guatemala. Finally, at Tulum, an old, walled port city facing the Caribbean, I said good-bye to Charles Kuralt and the CBS News crew who had accompanied me over much of the journey.

On July 17 I landed at Panama. I was feeling well and had gained back much of the weight lost in the preceding months. My illness had disappeared as mysteriously as it had begun; I was ready to go back to sea as soon as the hurricanes blew themselves out.

When I stepped out of the taxi at the old port of Panama and looked for the *Feathered Serpent,* she was nowhere to be seen. All my inquiries failed to locate her. She had simply disappeared without a trace. It was all quite mysterious.

The End of the Feathered Serpent

Upon my return to Peru I again made inquiries through official channels. It wasn't until the following year that I learned from my friend the Peruvian ambassador the details of what really had happened. The uncanny story can be told in a few words.

It seems that in July he had found the *Feathered Serpent* somewhat deteriorated and was arranging to have it shipped to Peru when a storm struck the harbor. After two days of heavy wind and rain, the balsa had disappeared.

In August it was sighted by an American naval vessel, far out at sea. It must have made a strange impression on the American sailors: a primitive craft, from a thousand years out of the past, sailing unmanned on the high seas, her colors flying. However, she was duly towed to the entrance of the canal and moored safely on the rocks of Fuerte Amador. By the time the ambassador learned where she had come to rest and arranged for her transport south, the balsa had vanished once again. This was in the month of October.

Thus ends the story of my expedition. The fate of the balsa is less certain. As though compelled by unknown forces to fulfill a mythological destiny, the *Feathered Serpent,* like her namesake, disappeared over the ocean, never to be seen again.

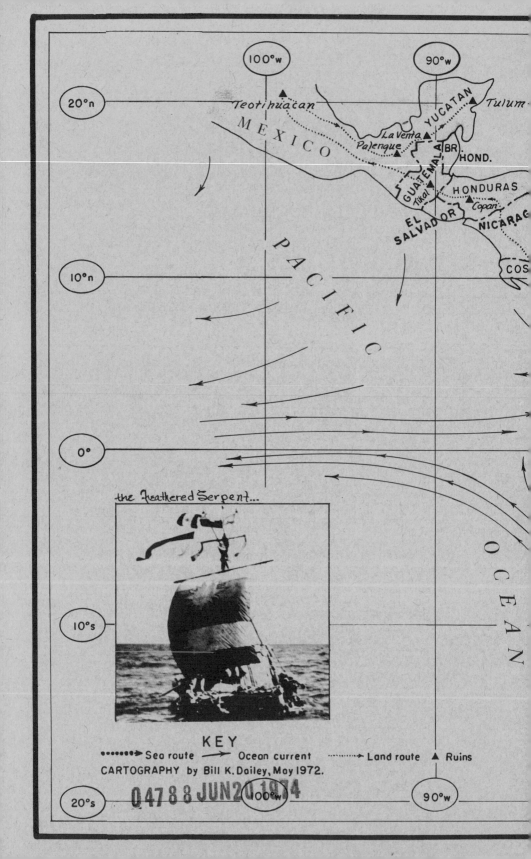

the Feathered Serpent...

KEY
●●●●●●→ Sea route   ⟶ Ocean current   ·······→ Land route   ▲ Ruins
CARTOGRAPHY by Bill K. Dailey, May 1972.